The Practical
Permaculture Project

The Practical
Permaculture Project

Connect to Nature and Discover the Best Organic Soil and Water Management Techniques to Design and Build your Thriving, Sustainable, Self-sufficient Garden

Written by Sophie McKay
www.SophieMcKay.com

Second edition, 2023

ISBN 978-1-7397356-0-9 (paperback)
ISBN 978-1-7397356-1-6 (ebook)
ISBN 978-1-7397356-2-3 (hardback)

Website: www.SophieMcKay.com
Email: Sophie@sophiemckay.com
Author page: https://www.facebook.com/Sophie.McKay.Author
Facebook: www.facebook.com/groups/garden.to.table.tribe

TABLE OF CONTENTS

Before we begin, go and grab your FREE gifts!

Sophie McKay's Seed starting & planting calculator
+ The Ultimate Guide to Organic Weed Management

In these free resources, you will discover:
- The perfect Seed Starting and Planting times for YOUR region or zone
- The 8 Organic Weed Removal Methods
- The 6 best and proven Weed Management Methods
- The tools you did NOT know you need for a weed-free garden
- How weeds can help your yard
- How to identify which weed is good and which is bad for a yard or garden
- The difference between Invasive and Noxious Weeds

Get your FREE copy today by visiting:
https://sophiemckay.com/free-resources/

Introduction

When I was little, gardening seemed like the most natural thing in the world to me. I grew up on my grandparents' farm, where a simple life was a happy one. My parents loved gardening so much they would take care in planting every seed or fruit tree we had around our yard. There were always flowers in our garden and fresh vegetables to eat, and soon enough, I had my first little herb garden of my own. It wasn't very big and didn't really last long, but growing up in that environment had such lasting effects on me, not least the love of cooking from fresh ingredients— the pride when you know what goes into your meal instead of eating factory-made foods with no flavor at all! And now here we are years later, after many mistakes—I'll never forget losing those zucchini plants—followed by lots of studies, experience, and successes.

During my studies and work, I traveled a lot and visited many countries. I recognized the positive impact sustainable agriculture was making on the environment and that's what drew me toward permaculture about ten years ago. I realized that permaculture is the way to grow food in harmony with nature using all available resources. It is the way to design and maintain food production systems that imitate nature and consequently thrive with nature's resilience, stability, and diversity. Permaculture integrates people and their land to provide them sustainably with food, shelter, energy, and other needs in the long term.

Permaculture asks us to turn to nature for inspiration and follow its relationships and patterns. Everything in an ecosystem is related, interdependent, and crucial for the health of the system.

Whenever I mention permaculture to someone who's never heard of it before, I always get to hear something along the lines of "That sounds like a lot of work" or "That sounds complicated; I could never do what you're doing." This makes me smile, because I had the same thoughts when I first started, and now I rarely ever go to the grocery store.

Your future sustainable garden in your own backyard allows you to take charge of your own food supply with minimal damage to the environment. While we will also touch on the social and cultural aspects of permaculture, the purpose of this book is to show you why permaculture can change the way you relate to nature as you grow food and develop independence from outside sources of food. It gives you such an empowering feeling when everything starts coming full circle and you are able to say: "I created this." I believe it's our responsibility as people with firsthand knowledge of the joys of gardening to pass this message along.

This book is filled with simple and easy-to-follow instructions to help you transform your backyard or any space available in your home into a flourishing vegetable or fruit garden to meet your food requirements. The joy that you get from harvesting your own fresh produce is incomparable, and it feels amazing discovering a way to work with nature to fulfill your family's needs.

You are about to read a detailed and practical guide for designing and developing your own permaculture garden, advice on how to deal with problems and issues you will encounter that might discourage you, and a simple, easy-to-understand plan of action for building your permaculture operation.

Regardless of the size of the plot of land you have to work with, your climate, your financial resources, and your gardening skills, following this book's straightforward advice will allow you to create the permaculture garden that will be the beginning of your future food independence.

The Practical Permaculture Project is a comprehensive guide to sustainable living that gives you more financial stability. The techniques you'll learn in this book help you gain confidence in your own abilities to keep your family well fed despite economic or environmental uncertainty. Like the father of permaculture, Bill Mollison, once said: "Though the problems of the world are increasingly complex, the solutions remain embarrassingly simple."

Whether you're an experienced gardener or an absolute beginner, you can build your own permaculture garden. My decade of experimenting with permaculture techniques has brought successes and mistakes that have taught me so much, and I want to share those lessons with you. With the practical tips in this book, you can get started today, and before you know it, you'll have a productive ecological system on your own doorstep.

So get rid of your fears and get down to gardening. Grow food, and you'll feel better than ever. It's time to find your green thumb.

CHAPTER 1

Getting Down to the Roots

As an avid gardener and a nature lover, I've so often sought refuge from my worries in the presence of my plants. Ever since I was young, I tried to find ways to surround myself with nature by taking long walks in the park or going hiking. As an adult, my house has always been filled with houseplants and I love spending time in the company of my little green friends. Despite the deep connection I shared with nature, it never occurred to me that I could turn my passion into a source of sustenance.

I discovered permaculture a few years ago and it changed my life. I was amazed to learn that not only could I grow my own food, but I could also gain financial stability just by doing what I always loved to do. But what drew me towards permaculture the most was that it could heal our planet by reversing the damage that we humans have inflicted on our environment.

For years, scientists have been ringing the alarm about climate change, but their warnings fall on deaf ears. As someone who's always found peace in the presence of nature, a grim thought crosses my mind sometimes: *What if one day we lose all the natural beauty that surrounds us?*

When I learned about permaculture almost ten years ago, I thought it was an ingenious idea to slam the brakes on rapid environmental degradation and improve our modern lifestyles with sustainable agricultural practices.

Moreover, permaculture has helped me to achieve economic stability and food security through working in harmony with nature. I know too well the anxiety of not knowing where your next meal will come from, having faced financial troubles in the past. Taking charge of my own food supply made me feel less anxious about the future. It gave me more control over my health, since I no longer had to rely on store-bought vegetables and fruits that have been treated with various chemicals to ward off unwanted insects and pests and increase yields.

I experienced tremendous change as I started living in a more sustainable and self-sufficient manner. I couldn't help but think that I had to share the knowledge I'd gained about sustainable living with others to help them gain empowerment.

I see people struggling to make ends meet, suffering from poor health due to food scarcity and low-quality food, and feeling uncertain about their future. Permaculture can help these people out of their misery and give them the tools to provide for themselves. So, what exactly is permaculture?

Imagine only having to walk a few steps out of your door and finding everything you need in your own backyard—ripe red tomatoes, fresh vegetables, and organic eggs to make a delicious omelet for breakfast or some pasta for dinner. Imagine all your food problems coming to an end and never having to worry about running out of money to buy groceries. Imagine being able to stock your fridge with healthy, delicious food that's free from any chemicals. You may think to yourself: *Could it be so simple?* The answer is a resounding "yes."

Permaculture involves studying the different patterns and systems of nature to devise a method of fulfilling our needs without upsetting other ecosystems or the environment at large. The term itself is a combination of two words: "permanent" and "agriculture." The idea was developed in the seventies by two Australians, Bill Mollison and David Holmgren, as a form of sustainable agriculture. The foundational knowledge was primarily collected from native/aboriginal groups from around the world. These groups worked with nature instead of fighting it and we have benefited greatly from their willingness to share their knowledge with us. Systems based on this idea mimic natural ecosystems and involve little to no primary input like chemical fertilizers and pesticides. Permaculture relies heavily on closed-loop systems, which involve methods such as recycling waste products to fulfill energy requirements, growing forage crops to obtain feed for livestock and using manure to enhance soil fertility. In all of the aforementioned processes, "primary input" is obtained as a result of one process and used to initiate the other.

The idea for permaculture came to Mollison in Tasmania in 1959 while he watched marsupials nibbling leaves and twigs in the rainforest. He found himself inspired and in awe of the interconnected nature and rich abundance of life. "I believe that we could build systems that function as well as this one does," he wrote in his diary. He paired up with Holmgren soon after and began identifying the principles of these systems. Together, they penned their now famous book, "Permaculture One."

Permaculture is essentially a way to repair the damage inflicted on the environment, by observing nature with a keen eye and detecting different ecological patterns. Water, soil, plants, and climate are critical elements of permaculture, and we need to observe these elements and study their interaction to develop successful permaculture farming techniques. Going out into your garden or patio and noting the weather, the direction of the wind and the amount of sunlight are simple ways to study natural patterns.

Bill Mollison defined permaculture as a method of constructing sustainable human settlements by design and ecology. He described it as a philosophy or an approach to use land in a way that connects animals, plants, soils, human needs, water, and microclimates that yields productive communities. As he summarized it: "Permaculture is working *with* nature rather than *against* it."

While permaculture has gained popularity over the years, many gardeners remain skeptical of this new trend. They don't understand how their neat little rows of vegetables fit into this wilder style of gardening. They feel apprehensive that by adopting permaculture, they won't be able to grow the big red tomatoes that they're so used to, and they wonder what will happen to their flower beds if they try to create a more natural landscape. In this book, I will show you why you don't need to worry about that. Our tendency to over-complicate matters is what prevents us from adopting a more sustainable way of living.

The ecological gardens created as a result of permaculture combine the best features of edible landscapes, vegetable and flower patches, and wildlife gardens. These gardens feel like living beings with unique characters, and they require only low maintenance to deliver low environmental impact and high yields. They strike the perfect balance between aesthetics and practicality.

To better understand permaculture, we have to get down to the roots and start with the basics.

A Solid Foundation: The Three Ethics

The following elements make up the basic framework of permaculture and play an essential role in creating sustainable agricultural systems or ecological gardens:

1. Care of the Earth

Permaculture is deeply rooted in respect for all life forms by preserving and honoring every life system and playing fair. Since everything in nature is interconnected, our survival depends on the health and survival of other systems on Earth.

2. Care of the People

Humans are central to the idea of sustainable living. Permaculture makes sure that everyone has access to the resources that are necessary for survival. It builds trust and cooperation between people to build healthy communities. Helping others is critical to ensuring our survival as well as the survival of the human species.

3. Fair Share

One of the fundamental concepts behind permaculture is to take no more than our fair share. The Earth's resources are finite, and we need to return what we take to make sure the Earth remains healthy.

Benefits of Permaculture

The benefits of working hand-in-hand with nature and taking no more than what we need are immense. Let's look at some advantages of permaculture, especially in urban areas.

1. Surrounding yourself with nature is beneficial for your mental health. It's no secret that a splash of green can instantly brighten up a dull home. Similarly, immersing ourselves in nature and surrounding ourselves with plants is extremely good for our mental health. Urban dwellers usually live in concrete jungles with a smattering of green patches in between; permaculture allows apartment owners and people living in small spaces with little land available for gardening to transform small patches of dirt into colorful

vegetable patches. Caring for plants creates a sense of ownership and pride as we see them thrive and flourish. The therapeutic nature of planting makes it an excellent soothing and comforting activity for recovering drug addicts and mental health patients, so you can only imagine its positive impact on ordinary people that just need a little pick-me-up.

2. Concrete surfaces in an urban setting create an "urban heat island effect" where concrete structures absorb heat and reach extremely high temperatures. Building small green spaces in your home can cut down your electricity bill. Plants on the roof, balcony, or in places that usually get a lot of harsh sunlight can soak up the heat and create a cooler atmosphere, so you don't feel the need to crank up the air conditioning.

3. The zero-waste approach of permaculture allows you to reduce your carbon footprint significantly. The shells of the eggs that you ate for breakfast can become an essential source of calcium for your plants, while fruit and vegetable waste can provide carbon and nitrogen to make your plants flourish.

4. Permaculture encourages planting local perennial plants, which boosts the local insect population. So you will end up with many vibrant and new plant varieties as these insects pollinate your plants.

5. Permaculture in urban areas improves air quality indoors. Experiments performed by NASA scientists confirm that plants can absorb many volatile organic compounds (VOC) such as formaldehyde, benzene, and trichloroethylene. Selecting the proper trees to use as hedges will suppress a wide range of sound waves and provide natural soundproofing in urban environments.

6. If you're sick of the constant buzzing of mosquitoes and tired of swatting at them, then permaculture could help provide long-term solutions to keep the tiny blood-sucking vampires away from your home. You can incorporate plants such as lemongrass and other herbs that keep harmful pests and insects. Also, having a little pond in your backyard will attract frogs to move in, which is a great way to fight mosquitos.

7. It cuts down food costs drastically. Imagine strolling to your backyard to pluck some basil and tomatoes for making spaghetti. Permaculture means fewer trips to the grocery store and more control over what you eat and how you grow it.

8. Taking charge of your food supply by employing permaculture techniques means the food that makes its way to your dinner is healthier and more flavorful than what you'll find at the store. On average, 30% of nutrients are lost from produce within three days of being harvested, and it's unlikely that the food that ends up in your grocery store made it there within three days. So, the food grown in your own permaculture garden tends to be more nutrient-dense than store-bought fruits and vegetables.

9. It helps you save on artificial fertilizer, as you turn trash into a source of essential nutrients for your plants. Moreover, permaculture encourages the use of effective microorganisms to improve plant soil, which can easily be introduced by composting household waste. Natural fertilizers such as homemade compost enhance the soil quality without using up a large chunk from your paycheck every month.

10. Permaculture brings people together and builds healthy, tight-knit communities. Individuals with extra land are encouraged to share it with others to give everyone access to

growing their own food. It gives communities a shared sense of purpose and direction that brings strangers closer together.

11. Permaculture shrinks transportation distances and helps cut down the emission of toxic gasses, thereby improving air quality. So, not only do you get to enjoy healthier food on your table, but you also get a sense of accomplishment for helping create a greener and healthier planet.

12. It teaches you to use your resources wisely and efficiently by using every single resource in a way that benefits humans, animals, or nature so that nothing goes to waste.

13. It encourages the use of renewable energy, pushing growers toward more sustainable options and making them self-sufficient in the process.

Challenges You May Face When Switching to Permaculture

All in all, permaculture is an excellent solution to many of our problems; however, we must anticipate and prepare for any difficulties we may encounter before committing ourselves to a new way of living. Here are some possible disadvantages of permaculture and their solutions:

1. Setting up the basic infrastructure of permaculture can take a toll on your savings. It can be somewhat costly to design sustainable systems from scratch, making it difficult for people who're short on cash to achieve sustainability. But, rest assured, once your permaculture setup becomes functional, you will earn and save more than you could ever imagine. Also, you can always start small and work your way up as you start making profits.

I started my permaculture journey with a single raised bed in my backyard. I used it to grow a number of vegetables, which weren't all a success. Instead of letting my failures hold me back, I took note of my mistakes and made sure not to repeat them. I introduced myself to my neighbors, invited them for tea, and we started swapping plants and seeds. They shared their experiences about local climate and native shrubs, and I helped them by building new beds and implementing water-saving ideas. Within a year, I had a flourishing vegetable garden and I installed a few more raised beds. The next summer, we had enough harvest to sell on the market. I started making simple pickles and dips (like pesto and tomato sauce for pasta), and the customers loved the homemade flavors.

Once the profits started rolling in, I moved to a bigger set up. During this time, I started to shift to renewable energy, minimized my expenses by establishing closed-loop systems and used my resources wisely. I was finally able to save enough to rent, and then to buy, a bigger piece of land and expand my permaculture garden significantly.

It doesn't cost much to build a few small raised beds on your patio or terrace and slowly expand your setup as you go along.

2. Permaculture is based on reaping long-term benefits at the cost of short-term gains. While long-term solutions sound logical, the long wait to see their investments materialize into profits can be difficult for some. However, don't let this dissuade you from building a permaculture setup on your property, because there are many different ways that you can shorten the waiting process and harvest your food quickly. Some methods include extending the growing season, growing a combination of perennial and annual varieties so that you have something to eat or sell during every season, and using basic permaculture principles to speed up the growth of your plants and the yield.

3. It can lead to pest and disease problems, since pesticides or chemicals to fight off bacteria, fungi, and insects are not allowed. However, I will show you in the upcoming chapters how these challenges can be easily controlled and avoided altogether using simple techniques such as drip irrigation, companion planting, spacing out your plants, and growing certain varieties of plants that repel harmful bacteria, fungi, and insects.

4. Some people think that the use of fewer machines means that more manual labor is required, making labor costs shoot up as farmers employ more workers. This may discourage you as a gardener from adopting permaculture, thinking that it's very physically demanding to do all the hard work by yourself. However, there are many ways that you can reduce the amount of labor involved in a permaculture garden, such as by making no-till gardens, building raised beds, installing a bamboo irrigation system, and building closely related setups near each other to maintain ease of access, such as placing a compost bin in the center of a vegetable garden and a chicken coop next to the vegetable garden so that you can easily transfer chicken manure to the garden.

While there are some downsides of permaculture, most of these problems that arise can be avoided through simple planning. By implementing permaculture principles and following good gardening practices, you can smooth out any issues that you may face while setting up your own permaculture garden.

It's an investment that takes time to mature but eventually pays off abundantly. With economic uncertainty looming large as the global population swells while food supplies struggle to keep up, permaculture offers a good alternative worth giving a shot.

The Practical Framework: The Twelve Principles of Permaculture

Permaculture is essentially a blueprint for sustainable living that is built on twelve principles. These principles complement the three basic elements of permaculture (care for the Earth, care for people, and fair share) and lay the groundwork for creating sustainable agricultural systems.

Principle 1
Watch and Learn: The Art of Observation

Observing and understanding nature can help us develop sustainable designs where different species coexist in harmony with the environment. It is crucial when designing sustainable gardens to take the time to observe the natural patterns in our surroundings. Learning about local plant populations, analyzing the soil on your land, and studying the waterways are essential to building a permaculture garden that's in harmony with nature. Researching local foods and supporting cuisine by growing ingredients that are commonly used is also great due diligence.

Many permaculturists recommend camping for up to a year on the piece of land where you plan to live to understand the place's natural rhythms. Close and detailed observation allows us to look at a whole system or problem, observe how the different parts relate, see connections between the key features, and ultimately apply ideas from long-term sustainable systems.

For example, observing the sun's movement during the different seasons and how it affects specific areas on the land where you live can help you determine how to angle your house or even your greenhouse to achieve the most solar energy and create microclimates for certain plants.

If you already have a garden set up in place, analyze the quality of the soil, which places stay under shade and which are the brightest, take note of the plants you already have growing and look for areas where they tend to grow well and the places where they don't. Even in a small garden, environmental factors such as wind, moisture, sunlight and soil fertility could vary greatly. These subtle variations add up to create different microclimates that can be used to your advantage to grow a number of different plants.

Principle 2
Make The Most of Your Resources

Our dependency on fossil fuels is detrimental for our planet. Permaculture teaches us to collect resources when they are plentiful and store them for when they are not. The most basic application of this principle is harvesting food to keep for the winter instead of depending on your local grocery store to fly fresh vegetables in from overseas.

Water is an important resource that you should use wisely. It is necessary for photosynthesis, which allows the plant to harvest energy from the sun. Finding ways to collect and store rainwater for the dry season is another essential application of this principle.

We can apply this principle in our everyday life. You might want to consider orientating your house or greenhouse so that it faces southward if you live in the southern hemisphere (northward if you live in the northern hemisphere). This way you can utilize the sunlight when it is low in the sky during winter to heat your home or prevent frost in your greenhouse. This will expand the growing season for your plants!

Remember that food is also a source of energy. Therefore, growing those foods that can be preserved (such as beans) and employing food preservation techniques such as canning and freezing is also an essential part of sustainable living. Similarly, time is also a resource and it should be spent wisely, making it necessary to maintain a healthy work-life balance.

Principle 3
Keep Profitability in Mind

Any agricultural activity is only worthwhile if it provides something in return for all of your work. Planting a whole farm in clover and hairy vetch may give loads of nitrogen to boost soil fertility, but if you don't get anything to eat from the land, then sooner or later, you'll run into a problem.

Obtaining a yield means that you are getting something back for the effort you put in. If one of your goals for your land's first-year management is to boost soil fertility before planting an orchard, then the yield from your clover and vetch field may very well be worthwhile.

Permaculture isn't simply a way to create wilderness or wild places. Instead, permaculture sees human beings as integral parts of the landscape whose needs must also be fulfilled without disturbing the rest of the system. Reconnecting with nature is an integral part of permaculture; therefore, studying natural cycles and incorporating them into your design is key.

Principle 4
Practice Self-Regulation: Learn and Refocus

We need to learn from our mistakes as well as from our successes. We may learn from experience the optimum number of chickens to pasture through our orchard. Too many and they may begin to leave the soil bare; too few and the weeds start to compete with our peach trees for nutrients. A large part of permaculture involves self-assessment, using setbacks as learning opportunities, and taking steps to minimize mistakes in the future.

Principle 5
Switch to Green Energy

We may live in an area that receives thousands of millimeters of rain every year but still decide to depend on a municipal water source that is unsustainably drawn from a local river or aquifer and pumped uphill at the expense of enormous amounts of water.

Our goal should always be to minimize our use of non-renewable sources of energy and services while maximizing our use of renewables within sustainable limits. This doesn't just apply to sources of energy and water but can be related to everything from which materials we use to build our house and how we fence our land. Our barbed wire and concrete post fence simply won't last as long as a good fence made from solid black locust seedlings.

Adopting renewable energy not only increases sustainability but also cuts the cost of running your agricultural setup considerably. Other ways that you can help save the planet and nature include using chemical-free household products and cutting back on the use of harmful chemicals for growing crops by opting for worm farming.

Principle 6
Recycle Waste Products

What we take from the system, we need to give back to it, and this is best done by getting rid of the concept of waste. It is simply senseless that millions of metric tons of organic material are buried in landfills every year when that could quickly turn that supposed "waste" into the fertility we need for our gardens.

Traditional Chinese farmers were famous for the use of "night soil." Every night, farmers would take their carts into the nearest city or village and load up human and animal excrement to spread over their fields at night, thus ensuring the long-term fertility of the land that sustained them.

The basis of this principle is that the output from one system is the input to the next system. The production from our bodies (and any animals we may keep) should be the input for soil fertility. This can be achieved through compost toilets, reuse of graywater (wastewater free from fecal contamination) and blackwater (wastewater from toilets), and composting kitchen scraps.

Principle 7
Learn About Your Local Climate

The vital permaculture design process shouldn't simply focus on what plant we want to grow or where we're thinking about placing our chicken coop. These details follow from a mindful and conscientious process of stepping back to observe larger patterns. These patterns then go on to form the base of our designs.

For example, by observing weather patterns, we may discern which parts of our land receive the most wind and plan to build our greenhouse accordingly. If we simply started from the detail of wanting a greenhouse somewhere on our land, we may very well end up erecting it in a place where the first significant wind storm will rip it to pieces. A great technique to achieve all this is to start a garden diary soon after devising your base map to learn more about the local climate, plant, and animal species.

Principle 8
Always Look at the Big Picture

The poet John Donne once said that "no man is an island"; we are all interconnected by an invisible thread. We may believe that what happens to other species doesn't affect us, but the reality is that everything on this planet is assembled like a row of dominoes. Using chemical pesticides might help you get rid of unwanted pests, but it can have a disastrous effect on the ecosystem by poisoning the entire food web. Extinction of one animal or plant species can disrupt the entire food chain, endangering other species; a process known as the "cascading effect".

Permaculture encourages us to always look at the picture as a whole instead of staying focused on ourselves and wondering how we fit into the equation. Get rid of tunnel vision and take a broad view of the situation. What effect will your actions have on others? What impact will your decisions have on the environment? How does your presence influence other plant and animal species?

Joining a community garden or permaculture group can help you connect with other like-minded people. Having strong community ties increases morale, confidence, and mental wellbeing. Learning to integrate different elements of life means helping to develop relationships between things that work well together. Instead of simply planting a bed of ten tomato plants, planting five tomato plants surrounded by some Mexican marigolds and a few basil or oregano bushes causes numerous symbiotic relationships to develop, improving the entire system.

Principle 9
Look for Simple Solutions

It's widely believed that the best solution to our problems is the fastest one. If we've got a problem with aphids in our apple orchard, then bring in the chemicals loaded into a 100-gallon mechanical sprayer hauled from the back of a heavy-duty tractor. Usually, we want our problem fixed in the most efficient manner. The problem, of course, is that efficiency isn't always the best solution. We also have to plan long-term and keep sustainability in mind.

Piling wood chips under our fruit trees can improve soil quality and tree resilience, while planting umbels and daisies to attract beneficial insects may be a better long-term solution to our apple orchard bug problem. Planting daisies and umbels in and around your vegetable garden will bring beneficial insects and pollinators, resolving most pest problems and increasing harvests through pollination. Daisy flowers attract larger insect pollinators such as bees, while umbels bring small native bees, as well as lacewings, parasitic wasps and hoverflies, which are fantastic pest-controlling predators. Pest populations that these insects help control include mites, mealybugs, aphids and botrytis.

However, it takes time to implement these ideas. Saving seeds and starting your own seed bank is also an ingenious technique to ensure you have a food supply in the future. Simple solutions allow better use of resources, and they also let us observe the effects of our actions and change course, if necessary.

Principle 10
Diversify: Increase the Health of Your Plants

Nowhere in the world will one find a naturally occurring monoculture. Diversity allows for more resilience, stability, and equilibrium in the long run. Planting one hectare of cabbage simply doesn't offer the strength or the security that comes with diversifying that hectare with thirty types of different crops strategically placed to maximize beneficial and symbiotic relationships. Boosting local pollinators such as bees, butterflies, and beetles is also a great way to increase plant diversity.

Principle 11
Don't Forget to Plant Along the Edges

The edges that exist between systems are usually the most productive and diverse areas. For example, by simply digging a pond somewhere on your land, the "edge" between the water and the ground will create a boom in diversity as hundreds of different species will find their way into this new niche in the landscape.

What many consider to be marginal land (an abandoned hedge, for example) could very well become the most diverse and productive part of your landscape with a bit of work and dedication. You have to think outside of the box and come up with creative ways to use your land by considering different factors.

Principle 12
Come Up with Creative Solutions and Adapt to Change

Change is inevitable and often ushers new possibilities if we are open to receiving them. Setbacks and obstacles are unavoidable; however, instead of worrying about the crises at hand, you need to learn to look at a situation from different perspectives and develop ways to turn things around in your favor. Problem solving lies at the heart of permaculture; it encourages you to adopt a positive mindset and look at failure as just another stepping stone.

Permaculture asks us to seriously observe the natural world, learn from it, and design our lives and landscapes accordingly. Its principles are grounded in nature's wisdom and are not just limited to agriculture. It focuses less on the objects involved and more on the unique relationships and intricate design between them that leads to healthy and sustainable systems. The interconnections between these objects makes the wheels turn and creates fully functioning systems, whether in your backyard, community, or ecosystem.

The concept of permaculture can be used to produce sustainable energy systems, design buildings, manage wastewater, build sustainable villages, create business models, and establish self-sufficient communities. The principles of permaculture trickle into several other aspects and encompass a wide array of practices that nudge us toward sustainability, such as renewable energy, organic gardening, recycling, community building, and social justice. So, permaculture is not a discipline in itself but a design approach that combines different strategies, fields, and techniques.

The twelfth principle of permaculture entails devising emergency plans to keep our agricultural system functioning in the worst circumstances. Shifting to renewable energy, preserving surplus food, using cold frames and heat traps and storing seeds are some innovative techniques that help us overcome obstacles and maintain a steady food supply all year long.

Most people see permaculture as a set of techniques. While there are some practices that embody the principles of permaculture accurately, such as keyhole beds and herb spirals, permaculture borrows ideas and techniques from a wide range of disciplines. These techniques are selected and applied based on their compatibility with permaculture principles, making room for novelty and creativity. So permaculture doesn't follow a strict action code, deviating from which could put your garden at risk. It is forever growing and assimilating other practices as long as they fit in with the basic framework.

What will help you achieve sustainability?

In addition to the twelve principles of permaculture given above, there are another five key factors that are crucial for achieving your agricultural sustainability. Let's have a look at each one of these because these small factors can make a big impact.

1. CLOSED-LOOP SYSTEMS

   Water, food, shelter, and money are widely considered vital resources, essential for comfortable living. Hardly any one of us views the trash can in our home as a precious commodity that's worth sparing a thought for. Suppose we hold our breaths and peek into the trash can in the kitchen; our untrained eyes may not find anything of value, and we may scrunch up our nose, lift the trash bag, tie it up and haul it outside where it would no longer assault our sense of smell.

It may not occur to us that we are, in fact, throwing away valuable resources worth thousands of dollars.

Most traditional agricultural practices employ open-loop systems that use up natural resources to satisfy human needs and generate large amounts of waste products that end up in landfills, polluting the soil. Resources constantly enter and leave these systems, and single-use items play a central role. In contrast, permaculture relies on closed-loop systems where everything we take is returned to the Earth and used to power the system once more.

If you're growing livestock, then plant forage crops and grains or use kitchen waste so you won't have to spend money on buying feed. Similarly, you could use livestock manure to fertilize crops instead of spending on chemical fertilizer. Permaculture also induces a problem-solving mindset. "You don't have a snail problem; you have a duck deficiency," says Bill Mollison. Come to think of it; ducks *do* love eating the snails that have been wreaking havoc on your crops.

2. PERENNIAL CROPS

Tilling the soil has traditionally been used to improve aeration, get rid of weeds, level the soil, and incorporate fertilizer and manure into the root zone. However, this age-old practice damages soil structure by speeding up surface runoff and resulting in soil erosion. So it's understandable that permaculturists are not too fond of tillage and encourage planting perennial crops instead. These plants are planted once and don't require any tillage.

The no-dig gardening method uses layers of organic materials such as straw, animal manure, kitchen scraps, and compost. The garden bed is filled with these layers forming a thick, flat composting system. Holes or small pockets can be made in the garden bed to plant seedlings. This simple technique gives incredible results. In a nutshell, the no-dig garden is made of layers of carbon and nitrogen-rich materials, similar to a compost heap.

Covering exposed areas with a good layer of mulch protects the surface, helping the soil retain moisture and preventing erosion. This blocks sunlight, preventing the growth of weeds. Moreover, natural mulch gradually breaks down, releasing nutrients and adding organic matter to the soil, making it more fertile.

3. MULTIPLE FUNCTIONS

You'd be hard-pressed to not come across a multifunctional product being sold in an infomercial while flicking channels on the TV. We love a nifty little tool that gets two things done instead of just one, but why don't we think the same when it comes to agriculture? Imagine a fence that not only contains the animals but also functions as a windbreaker, trellis, or a reflective surface, bouncing off sunlight to reduce or enhance light and heat for your plants. You can also store rainwater in rain barrels and use it to water your plants when the skies clear. You might even use the water collected in these barrels to grow aquatic food plants and fish. Using a single resource in more ways than one like this is known as "stacking functions." In chapter 3, the illustration 3.2 shows how a food forest can simultaneously serve as a windbreak.

4. WATER CONSERVATION

Permaculture may sound like a relatively new concept, but many of the techniques that it employs have been around for a long time. The Aztecs came up with an ingenious design for crop irrigation known as *chinampas* that featured a system of canals and berms (barriers created around the edge of a water body that resemble mounds of soil) for growing crops and fish. Other methods for saving water and utilizing every single drop include building terraces on steep land and swales on land that slopes slightly. Terraces look like steps of a staircase, while swales are level ditches that collect runoff rainwater.

The figure 1.1 below illustrates how runoff water can be collected in swales where it sinks into the earth where it can be accessed by trees during a drought.

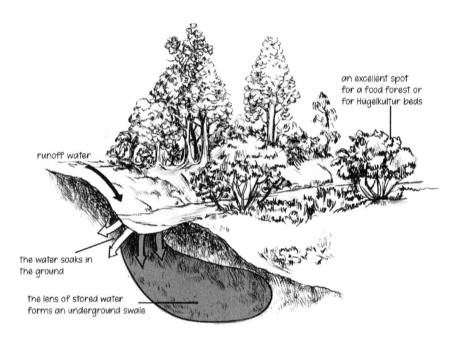

Figure 1.1: Storing water underground.

5. WORK WITH NATURE

Traditional methods of growing plants and livestock can sometimes feel like an uphill battle as farmers fight it out with nature. Permaculture is all about working alongside nature. It involves observing nature, studying the patterns and cycles that connect different lifeforms, and using the information for our benefit. For example, instead of keeping the hens cooped up in pens, let them run loose on land where you're going to plant crops so they can feast on the bugs and pests. Not only would you end up with well-fed hens, but you'd also get rid of pests that could harm your plants.

In the same way, you can plant *mashua* under a locust tree. The locust tree provides nitrogen to the soil, while the *mashua* plant is a vine that requires a support structure to climb. Planting locust trees eliminates the need for adding fertilizer to the soil, provides a trellis, and offers shade and food for bees.

We can have a thriving garden and healthy livestock with minimal effort by letting nature do its thing rather than getting in its way.

Permaculture is a powerful tool through which we can create a more sustainable future. Now that you know precisely what permaculture is and how it can be used to change our lives for the better, let's look at how our planet is changing and how permaculture can help us adapt to a future that will look very different from the present. Chapter 2 is all about keeping up with the changing times and using permaculture to make our way into the future.

Chapter 2

Permaculture:
A Necessity for Our Future

Apart from gardening, I love to travel. I've witnessed incredible beauty during my globetrotting adventures; however, it is disheartening to see how irresponsibly we treat nature all over the world. It's as if we've forgotten how closely our future is tied to nature and how the rapid destruction of natural resources and landscapes could make it difficult for future generations to survive. Thousands of acres of rainforest and scrubland are being cleared and flattened to make room for monocultures. Of course, this activity comes at the cost of losing precious wildlife as well.

While a wealthy few add to their profits by burning ecosystems and pumping out produce, many in society struggle to provide food for themselves and their families find themselves sliding further into poverty. As a result, we see people going hungry in places that should be teeming with food, places where the land is fertile and the weather excellent for growing crops, where no one should ever have to worry about finding something to eat.

You might feel skeptical at this point and wonder what people going hungry on the other side of the planet has to do with you. You have the convenience of getting food delivered to your doorstep with just one call if you feel the need. You won't be going hungry any time soon, so why worry?

While I understand why some people may feel cynical about sustainable living, the fact remains that climate change is a reality and sooner or later we are going to run into a major food crisis worldwide. Moreover, even though food shortage is not a first-world problem, being well fed does not mean that we're healthy.

A friend of mine, a retired cardiologist, recalled a somewhat amusing incident a few years ago at a conference. When the meeting ended, the speaker asked the audience a simple question: "Is dairy healthy or unhealthy?" The room, full of top cardiologists, fell silent, and he finally received a mixed response. The confusion prompted him to wonder why we don't have a definite answer for something as simple as diet, despite the incredible progress that we've made in science. "Why is there so much confusion about what to eat and what not to eat?" he asked.

Overfed but Malnourished

With obesity on the rise, it's hard to believe that people still suffer from nutrient deficiencies. We have a myriad of calorie-rich and nutrient-fortified options available, and still we continue to suffer from poor health. A 2002 study published in the *Journal of the American Medical Association* found that it is not unusual to find vitamin deficiency in Western countries, which can cause many chronic problems.

Another study published in the *Journal of Obesity Surgery* found that nutrient and mineral deficiencies could exist in morbidly obese people. Moreover, 2010 research published in the Clinical Journal of Sports Medicine found that even athletes could suffer from vitamin deficiencies.

So, why exactly are so many of us nutrient deficient when food is abundant? The answer always reminds me of a family Christmas party that I attended as a young child. I remember gathering around the Christmas tree with my cousins, going through all the presents, reading the names, and guessing what gift was inside. A large box in the corner of the room caught my eye, and I went up to it to see if it had my name on it. I was disappointed to find my uncle's name on the biggest, heaviest gift in the room and sulked for the rest of the evening until it was time to open all of the presents. You can imagine my surprise and relief when the gift turned out to be a large box stuffed with socks and weighed down with rocks. Turns out, one of my other uncles had decided to play a practical joke.

We can use the above story as an analogy to explain what's going on when we pack on the pounds but miss out on nutrients. Imagine that the box is the appearance of the food while the socks are the nutrient and mineral content. So, while there is no food shortage in developed countries, food quality has rapidly declined. The reason that our food lacks much-needed nutrients comes down to the Earth and how we treat it.

Over the past century, the topsoil in Canada and America has lost 85% of its mineral content. A 2004 study compared USDA nutrient content data from 1950 to 1999 in garden crops and found that depleted soil nutrient content has led to a 6% - 38% reduction in vitamin and mineral content (Davis et al., 2005).

Not only has our food lost a significant amount of nutrients, but we have also engineered new plant varieties that are loaded with chemical toxins. Glyphosates are common herbicides used to suppress weed populations; the use of these chemicals increased 15 times after genetically modified crops made their way to the market in 1994. Glyphosates are regularly sprayed on genetically modified crops that are themselves glyphosate resistant. Other crops like oats, wheat, and beans must be sprayed just a few days before harvest to dry out the plants, making it easier to harvest them earlier. Pre-harvest application of the herbicide leaves much higher residue of glyphosate in foods.

Vast differences in food supply exist across the world. While people living in one corner of the Earth go hungry, people in another corner face problems arising from an abundance of food, such as obesity. With the effects of climate change looming large, the unequal distribution of wealth and nutrition will only grow more intense. So even though our tables are overflowing with food, we continue to suffer from poor health. Our food has been tampered with and filled with harmful chemicals.

All this is enough to make you lose your appetite for dinner, but don't toss out the food on your plate just yet. There's a high chance that the food supply of the Western countries will also take a hit soon.

Effect of Climate Change

When it comes to climate change, we're at the edge of the precipice. The effects of climate change are going to affect agriculture and fisheries all over the world. A decrease in water availability, more frequent extreme weather events, increases in temperature, and changes in precipitation patterns will cause reduced agricultural productivity. Frequent severe weather episodes will also affect food delivery, resulting in increased food prices, while increased temperatures may cause food spoilage and contamination. Maybe you have experienced some of these events recently and understand very well that you need a long-term, sustainable food source to rely on.

While moderate warming and a slight increase in carbon dioxide may help some plants grow fast, a sharp rise in temperature and rapid weather fluctuations will ultimately harm crop yield. Reduced food supply, drought, and heatwaves may put livestock at risk as well. Changes in water temperatures could cause fish and shellfish species to change their habitat, disrupting entire ecosystems in the process.

Fortunately, people are becoming increasingly aware of the dire consequences of climate change and trying to find methods of surviving frequent natural disasters and economic collapse in the near future. A major shift is happening worldwide as more people realize that we can't go on living the way that we are much longer. We need to start turning to smart, sustainable farming solutions. However, while more people are waking up to the reality of climate change and there have been some large-scale efforts to bring attention to the climate crisis (such as the 2016 Paris Agreement and COP22), serious mass commitment and resolve to reverse the damage are still missing.

Permaculture: The Way Forward

We can feel the effects of soil erosion, low-quality food that lacks essential nutrients, and climate change right now, but these problems – if we don't change – will only get worse for future generations. Our children may not have the luxury of ignoring the disastrous consequences of our recklessness.

I know that you're worried about the future, and I know how it feels to find yourself utterly helpless in front of forces much bigger and stronger than yourself. Learning about the problems that lie in store for us in the future, you may wonder what you could do about it. Where do you start?

I know how you feel, because a few years ago, I was standing at the same place that you are, feeling vulnerable and insecure. I could go on and on about all that is wrong with the world and how we treat nature, but it won't help fix anything. I finally realized that if I wanted to make a change, I had to start with myself first and then invite others to change.

A few years ago, I visited the Maya Mountain Research establishment (MMRF) in Belize. During my trip, I also got the chance to see a tropical food forest. I found it fascinating that both projects were built on lands where traditional farming practices had eroded the soil, resulting in a significant drop in incomes. The projects proved to be productive by utilizing renewable energy and off-grid sanitation. As I witnessed the remarkable things these two projects had achieved, I realized the broad scope of permaculture and how we can use it to heal our planet.

Erratic weather patterns and an unpredictable future should be a source of worry for most of us. Sadly, not much is being done about climate change globally. However, there is a lot that we can do on an individual level to secure our future, prepare for an impending food crisis and ensure food and economic security for our children.

There is one clear way to begin to solve our current and future food problems: We must start growing our own food. Permaculture lets you take back ownership of what you eat. You no longer pack unknown chemicals and toxins in your body by consuming store-bought food that's been heavily chemically treated to improve yield. You're also able to save money by adopting self-sufficient farming techniques.

I'm here to help you on your journey by guiding you through key steps. The rest of the chapters in this book will teach you how to set up a permaculture garden or farm to overcome the limitations and drawbacks of modern society. It doesn't matter where you live or how much land you have. By the time you finish reading this book, you'll know how to make any piece of land fertile to grow your own food.

I want you to feel empowered and responsible for your future rather than feeling like a victim who has no control over what happens. The next chapter is all about planning your garden and how to start taking the first steps toward sustainable living. You'll learn what you need to get started and how you can successfully build a permaculture garden in your backyard.

CHAPTER 3

Plan Your Garden

Whether it's a small, barren piece of land, a dry patch of soil in your backyard, or desolate farmland, you can turn it into a blossoming garden through permaculture. One of the main tenets of permaculture is observing nature at work and replicating its design. Some experts suggest camping out in a field or spending some time in nature to quietly study its patterns, but if all that seems too much, simply becoming mindful of your surroundings and connecting with the nature around you can be an incredible learning experience.

You have learned by now that permaculture is about more than just producing large quantities of food. Permaculturists are more concerned with achieving abundant yields of healthy, nutritious food in ways that help regenerate damaged landscapes. Healing the land while increasing the quantity and quality of the food grown is one of the fundamental characteristics of permaculture design, so it's no surprise that coming up with a good plan is critical for success.

Permaculture design depends on certain prime directives based on the twelve principles of permaculture, which we've already discussed in the previous chapter. Let's have a look at some of these factors below.

Observe and Replicate

To become fully aware of our surroundings, we have to use our five senses thoughtfully. I've come across so many people who, despite having lived in the same place for years, are surprised when I point out a particular tree to them or tell them that the soil in their backyard is fertile or dry. "I had no idea that was there," they'd say, looking over at the tall tree that I'd shown them. Only when we use our senses of taste, smell, hearing, and touch fully do we become aware of everything in our surroundings.

Through close observation, you can find existing patterns in nature and use them to your advantage. Keep Bill Mollison's advice in mind and work with the land, not against it. For example, if you notice a slight breeze coming up every evening, maybe it would carry moisture, so you don't need to water the plants so much, or it could be drying and cause damage to the crops, so you might want to plant a hedge. Another useful pattern is the movement of the sun in different seasons. If you know which parts of your garden would be under shade or sunlight at different times of the day, then you can select the right plants that would thrive under those conditions.

Relative Location

We know that everything is connected, so it is imperative to choose the best placement relative to the surroundings to ensure the needs of each element or system. For example, the edge of the woods where foxes dwell is probably not the best place for a chicken coop. Similarly, starting a vegetable garden in a marshy area is only going to lead to more problems. In permaculture design, where we place each element in the landscape is extremely important and needs to be well considered.

The Functions of Each Element

Each element in your landscape (or garden) design should have as many functions as possible. If you're going to take the effort to put something onto your site, it needs to be worth the while. Think about how to get the most from every element on your land and place it accordingly. For example, a tree could be nothing more than a tree if planted arbitrarily without any forethought. However, when strategically placed, a tree offers shade, wind protection, food for humans, forage for animals, leaf fall for mulch, fertility for the soil (if it's nitrogen-fixing), etc.

Function Redundancy

It's never wise to put all your eggs in one basket, and similarly, every process needs to have multiple elements to keep the function fail-safe. For example, a spring near your house should not be your only source of water, because the spring water could dry up during a drought, become contaminated by a neighbor spraying pesticides uphill from the spring, or any other number of scenarios. Having an alternative second or third water source is imperative to keep the "function" of water availability reliable and guaranteed.

Growing Plants in Different Seasons and Climates

I was a bit apprehensive about starting permaculture in a temperate climate zone. The changing seasons brought with them different conditions, and I wondered whether the plants would be able to adjust to frosts, dry and wet seasons. I had to learn which plants could handle the cold and which were more suited to the warm summer months. I also realized the importance of hoop houses, cold frames, and various other methods to keep the temperature warm without using any fuel.

Hoop houses are portable greenhouses made with PVC pipes and plastic sheets. They can be used to speed up the growth of seedlings, extend harvest times and protect plants from extreme weather conditions such as scorching heat, heavy rain and snow. A cold frame is simply a rectangular, transparent frame that protects plants from cold weather while letting in sunlight.

Permaculture encourages plant growers to follow nature's lead and grow crops that are well suited to the climate of the location where we live. Dark, leafy green vegetables are an excellent pick for winter gardens. Vegetables such as spinach and kale lose their bitterness and become more flavorful when grown in frosty conditions. Lettuce, chard, arugula, cabbages, and endive are other varieties that grow well in winters.

Plants may suffer from heat stress under extremely hot weather. Luckily, there is a lot that you can do to save your plants from the scorching sun. The strategic placement of shading devices such as a fence can shield the plants from heat stress. Lightweight cloth, like old sheets, can also be used to block out the sunlight and create shade by tying the corners to a stake or wood. You can also buy shade cloth at your local garden center; a 6 x 12 ft of cloth can block 50% of light. Old window screens are also a great option, as are narrow wood panels of wood lattice. If the plants are too tall, you can use a screen to cover their base from the harsh afternoon sun.

Study the climate in your location and think of ways to use it to your advantage. Another excellent technique to increase plant yield is season extension, which utilizes the period when seasons blend into one another. As summer transitions into autumn, the days become shorter while the night stretches longer. The warm summer breeze makes way for biting cold winds, the leaves begin to fall, and fruiting happens less frequently. Unlike traditional farmers or gardeners, permaculturists don't pack up their tools during this time and start preparing for winter—the change of the season is seen as an opportunity.

You can prolong the growing period of high-value summer crops by a few weeks or months through season extension. The use of hoop houses and cold frames for tomatoes and peppers will keep them ripening despite the arrival of autumn. Similarly, you can vary harvesting times by selecting perennial fruits, herbs, and nut plants so that you have access to fruits and nuts in the later seasons.

Zone and Sector Analysis

Zone and sector analysis are a fundamental part of your design process. Sector analysis helps us overview different energies, like the wind, the rain, the sun, the risk of fire, the water flows, and the slope of the land, which could potentially affect crops and livestock. It can also include other factors such as a panoramic view of the landscape (yes, beauty is also important in permaculture design), the part of your land where wild animals most often pass through, etc. For example, knowing the direction of the warm summer sun and the cold winter winds will help you decide where you need to install a windbreak, how much sunlight different areas in your garden, patio or balcony receive and which places are covered with shade.

Remember, the size of land that you have to work with should not stop you from building a permaculture set up. Plants such as peppers, green onions, eggplants, tomatoes, radishes and beans are ideal candidates for urban gardening on patios and balconies.

Zone planning helps you decide the location of every element on your site based on how often you need to use the element and how much you need to invest in it to keep the element working in your favor. The parts you use most often or that require the most attention should be placed closest to your house, so you can access them easily, while the elements that require less human intervention and that would be used less frequently can be put farther away. For example, it's a good idea to build your kitchen garden close to your home so that you can easily harvest vegetables and herbs for your everyday meals. This proximity will allow you to better care for the vegetables, which tend to be high maintenance, and avoid having to walk to some remote corner of your land to pick some basil for your evening pasta dinner.

The primary purpose of a forest is wood production, so it can be placed farther from the house. There is considerably less day-to-day upkeep involved in maintaining a forest and you only need to visit it sparingly for routine maintenance, maybe on a weekly or monthly basis.

Zones are numbered from 0 to 5, with zone 0 being your actual house. These zones often blend into one another and the delineation between zones is very rarely visible. Let's explore different permaculture zones in more detail.

ZONE 0

Your living space is marked as Zone 0 and your house should be positioned in a way that makes it energy-efficient and where it can offer functions other than simply serving as a dwelling place. For example, angling your house to face south (in the northern hemisphere) to take advantage of the sun's energy is making your house much more energy-efficient. Placing it high up on the slope of your land will allow you to catch and store rainwater and distribute it by gravity throughout your land.

ZONE 1

This zone is usually the area closest to your house. This is the most intensively used zone that needs heavy management. In this zone, you would place elements that you access most often or elements that need your most frequent attention. Some possible elements include a small kitchen garden, small fruit trees, a worm farm to process kitchen waste, propagation areas, sheds, rainwater tanks, fuelwood storage, and living quarters for small animals such as rabbits. Since this area is generally small, the soil is usually created through heavy mulching and the irrigation system can be of a type that requires substantial human intervention, such as drip irrigation. For many people living in urban areas with a small backyard, zone 1 may encompass the majority of your available land.

Zone 2

This zone is still heavily used, but less intensively than the elements placed in zone 1. In this zone, you may include a small fruit or nut orchard, compost bins, a chicken coop, a small barn, a larger market garden for vegetables, and perennials that have longer growing seasons. Usually spot mulching is better than complete mulching (for example around the trees in an orchard) to maintain soil fertility.

Zone 3

This zone is what is most often considered to be farmland. It is usually a larger piece of land located a bit farther from the house where the main crops are grown (both for home use and for the market).

Pasture for animals is also a part of zone 3 if you choose to have animals on your site. Once established, these areas take less of your time to maintain, except at harvest time. Other elements in this zone could include larger orchards, grain crops, pastures for large livestock, dams or ponds for water storage, beehives, etc. Since this is a considerably larger area, creating soil is best done through the use of green manures and cover crops and irrigation may be from the rain only.

ZONE 4

This area is a semi-wild area that is still managed by humans. It is usually a wooded area or perhaps a planned forest ecosystem that offers things such as wild foods (like morel mushrooms), timber, firewood, and animal forage. The management of these forests (or grasslands if you live in the prairies) is usually achieved through browsing animals through the forest or managing saplings and undergrowth.

ZONE 5

This zone is meant to be an unmanaged area on your site, kind of like your own miniature wilderness conservation area. For people with lots of acreage, this may be the main part of your land. For others with nothing but an acre or two, zone 5 may be a small corner of wetland at the edge of your site. It is always important to leave some area on your land free from human intervention in order to discover what nature would do on your land. It is an opportunity for us humans to surrender our desire to want to control every part of "our" land and allow ourselves to learn from the natural cycles of nature.

Now that you're familiar with different zones, I'd like to invite you to play a little game that will help you understand this concept better. On the next page, you'll find an illustration that I prepared for you. Use this image to help you identify different zones. Read the descriptions above, if you need help and draw the zones on the illustration. When you feel confident enough, draw a map of your property on a blank piece of paper and mark the different zones.

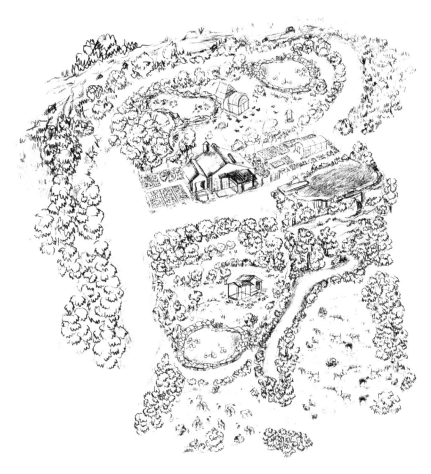

Zone 1: High-intensity area: herbs, herb spiral, raised beds, keyhole bed, garden beds, salad greens, dwarf fruit trees, flowers, greenhouse

Zone 2: Berries, chicken coop, pond, little fruit, and nut food forest

Zone 3: Larger fruit and nut trees, dams, swales

Zone 4: Forest for wild foraging and firewood, beehives, large livestock (horses, cows) meadow

Zone 5: Wilderness conservation area: creek, swamp, forest

Figure 3.1: Zone map.

Step-By-Step Guide for Designing a Permaculture Garden

Now that we've familiarized ourselves with the different zones in permaculture, let's discuss the different steps involved in setting up a permaculture garden.

Once you've checked off all the prerequisites of designing your own permaculture garden, it's time to get started on bringing your imagination to life. Here is a step-by-step guide to help you avoid pitfalls and successfully build a self-sustaining garden to satisfy all your needs.

STEP 1: LOOKING AT THE BIGGER PICTURE

Take a step back and look at the big picture. As I mentioned before, permaculture design depends on thoughtful observation of nature, recognizing different patterns, and studying the interactions of different elements. Here are some techniques to help you understand exactly what you need to observe to build the perfect permaculture garden.

Permaculture Observation Techniques and What to Observe

It is not possible to "observe" nature during a half-hour walk over your landscape or future garden site. To truly understand the rhythms, patterns, and reality of the place where you are going to live, you'll have to familiarize yourself with your land more intimately.

Ideally, it would be great to spend a year living on your land (or near it) before making any major changes to the site. During this time, you would be able to see the ebb and flow of the seasons and how temperatures change, as well as to study wind patterns and wildlife around your site. Witnessing the cyclical rhythms of nature over a whole year will allow you to make important design decisions to blend your life and livelihood with natural ecosystems. You will also discover how to take better advantage of the natural forces that are at your disposal.

For instance, if you live in the northern hemisphere, where cold winters will be something you'll have to consider when building a house, spending the first winter as an observer will allow you to see just how low the sun gets on the southern horizon and find those places on your site that receive the most light. Maybe the perfect place for you to set up your house is next to a huge cedar tree that will be blocking the winter sun, so you'll need to cut it down for lumber during the construction process. By observing the position of the sun in the winter sky, you'll be able to design your living space in a way that takes full advantage of passive solar design to heat your house without depending on a central heating unit that runs on fossil fuels (we will discuss this in more detail in the following chapters).

Experiencing the weather and surrounding environment at the place where you intend to set up your permaculture garden helps you make wise decisions by taking into account the unique conditions of that land. For example, imagine purchasing a piece of land in an area that gets flooded by over a hundred inches of rain each year. The site is sloped on all four sides surrounding a flat area in the middle, making it almost bowl-shaped. You might have looked forward to growing a garden in the flat area of the land because of the fertile topsoil that had accumulated over years of erosion from the surrounding hillsides. During the first growing season, you could plant dozens of different types of vegetables, but after a month of heavy rain, the flat bottom of the site will become a soggy bog and the majority of the vegetables will be ruined.

By watching how the rain affects the land during the rest of the wet season, you could have changed your design approach. Once the rains slowed down, you could begin to dig a series of swales (on contour ditches) to retain water and build "hügelkultur" beds with raised edges to control the flow of water and stop soil erosion. During the next rainy season, you could cautiously plant a small vegetable garden and watch as the rains, instead of washing into the flat bottom of the land, accumulate in the swales and get absorbed by the hillside slopes. The flat bottomland may not get flooded, allowing the vegetable garden to prosper, while the soil on the slopes begins the long process of rebuilding fertility.

City lots can be tricky, because they're often surrounded by tall buildings on all sides. By spending some time observing how the buildings block the sun and shade certain areas of the site, you can discover the best relative location for each type of plant that you'll be trying to grow. For example, if there is a corner of the lot that is almost always covered in shade, consider planting some currants there or perhaps some leeks, both of which thrive in partial to full shade. Save the sunny areas of the lot for growing tomatoes and peppers.

The Development of Peripheral Vision

Most of us never realize that we have various "types" of vision. The most common vision that we use on a day-to-day basis is our tunnel vision, where both eyes focus on one specific object.

Tunnel vision is important; however, it can also be limiting. It keeps us from tripping as we walk down the sidewalk and helps us to focus directly on the object of our sight, while peripheral vision will allow us to take into consideration a more complete picture. Many times, by focusing only on one specific object, we miss out on all the other "background" elements that are in play. Permaculture design urges us to take into account all of those background elements that many times we don't see.

Developing our ability to enter into peripheral vision allows us to shift our attention onto the shapes, colors, textures, and motions perceived through our sight. Peripheral vision also allows us in a sense to silence the chatter in our mind and to break the habit of directly focusing on everything seen.

One great practice for developing a peripheral vision is to find a spot in some wild area such as a small forest, a prairie, or even a park in an urban area. First, let your tunnel vision take over. Observe how your attention jumps from one object to the other. Then, put both of your hands directly in front of your face, about three inches from your eyes. Focus on the palms of your hands and then slowly remove your hands while making an effort not to focus on anything in particular once your hands are out of your sight. You may feel like you're not "seeing" anything, but be patient and let your mind adjust to the wider angles that peripheral vision allows.

As you develop your peripheral vision, you will be able to focus on more than one object. For example, in a forest or prairie, you might begin noticing the subtle movement of insects and birds that your tunnel vision didn't allow you to see. In a sense, tapping into your peripheral vision makes the forest come alive. You may even sense the movement of light filtering through the canopy of leaves above and discover small animals like squirrels skittering over the tree trunk, which you may not have noticed before.

Developing peripheral vision can be difficult at first, but it is a great observation tool to help you slowly develop an understanding of how different elements interact within your site.

STEP 2: TAKE A LONG WALK IN THE RAIN

I understand that not everyone has the luxury of waiting an entire year to observe how the interactions of the elements affects every aspect of their site. If you are a bit impatient, or if your life is too busy, there are other ways to observe and learn about the place where you plan to live that will help you become more aware of the different elements and how they work together to create a natural system.

One of the easiest and most important things you can do is plan to be on your site during a good rainstorm. Most people run for cover when it rains, and don't get to see what the rain does to the land. One of the most important practices of permaculture that we'll discuss later on in this book is to slow the movement of water, spread it over the land, and let it sink into the soil.

When it rains, get your boots and rain jacket on and walk through the land. Observe the places on your site where the water is accumulating. You may find a good place for a small pond or you may need to make some earthworks to stop that accumulation. Walk to places on your land where there is a slope and see how the water rolls down. Is it washing away valuable topsoil, creating rivulets that could ruin your farm? If so, you may have to put in some contour swales or some berms to slow the water and let it seep into the land. Observe how the water behaves on the site where you plan to construct your house. It should flow away from this site, but if you see water accumulating then you'll have to take this into account and prepare when you begin building your house.

Water is a crucial element for any permaculture design, but when its effects are simply ignored, water can be extremely damaging to the landscape. Through careful observation, however, you can come up with a good design that makes the most of this essential force of nature.

STEP 3: THE FIRST QUESTIONS ABOUT ENERGY AND RESOURCES

Below you will find a short questionnaire that can help you get started on the process of designing your site. These questions should lead you to other questions that are more site-specific and will help you get down to precise details about your land. Make notes—they will help you to set up the optimal plan

- From where does the sun enter your landscape? How many hours of sun do you receive on average? Does your site allow you to position solar panels for maximum solar gain?

- Is your site located in a place that receives lots of wind? How could you utilize that source of energy and mitigate it's potential for damaging your home?

- Do you have access to electricity on your site? If not, how will you go about heating and cooling your home? Even if you do have access to the electric grid, could you supplement your energy use or remodel your home to allow for other sorts of more ecological energy sources?

- What about refrigeration and freezing? How will you preserve your harvests?

- What else exists in abundance on your land? While this may initially be considered to be a negative characteristic of the land, is there any way to change it into a positive?

- How can you make use of this abundant element and what can you accomplish to benefit yourself, your crops, and your livestock?

POWERING UP: FINDING MULTIPLE SOURCES OF ENERGY

As we have seen, permaculture offers a unique perspective of design for urban areas as well as rural areas. Whether you inherited a forty-acre farm in the countryside or are trying to start a rooftop garden in downtown Chicago, finding the right technology is another element that needs to be taken into consideration in every permaculture design.

If you look at a permaculture layout more closely, you may find yourself wondering if you could generate your own energy. The answer is a resounding YES! Let's have a look at different energy sources that you can use.

Photovoltaic Cells

For several decades, scientists have been searching for ways to make solar cells more cost-effective and efficient. Researchers have been trying to develop new technologies to capture more light and increase its conversion into electricity. Photovoltaic cells are low cost machines that use solar panels to break light into different wavelengths.

In simple words, the light is split into different colors. The colored rays are then focused on a solar panel which converts light into electricity. This way a large amount of electricity is generated from colors with shorter wavelengths. With this new technology, we can utilize solar energy to support sustainable agriculture by helping farmers and plant growers save money, become self-reliant and reduce pollution. It provides an excellent solution for energy generation in remote locations. By using photovoltaic cells, we can harness energy from the sun and reduce our carbon footprint.

Wind Turbines (Eolic Energy)

Smaller wind turbines can help you generate electricity on a home level. A combination of wind and solar hybrid electricity generation systems can make the process more efficient.

Some people may find it surprising that the windmills dotting the rural landscapes in the past weren't used for energy generation, but to pump water. In the mountains, farmers put in a series of several windmills that would pump water to a tank on the high part of the watershed which was then distributed to the homes across the landscape.

Earth Tubes

Earth tubes, also known as ground-coupled heat exchange systems, are designed to take advantage of the cold air beneath the house to keep it comfortable during the worst heat waves. Ground temperatures just a few feet below our feet are usually comfortable at fifty to seventy degrees Fahrenheit. A ground heat exchange system requires water to be piped through a complex system, while a simple grounded pipe system requires a plastic PVC pipe and a small fan.

The entrance to the ground pipe system is a pipe protruding from the ground somewhere outside the house. At least a hundred feet of pipe goes under the base of the house and is buried a few feet underground until it penetrates the house. You can then branch these tubes in different directions so that the tube system leads to different rooms that you want to keep cool during the summer. Blowers are located at the entrance of the ground plumbing system to move air into the house through the plumbing system.

By burying a long plastic pipe under the ground, the cold temperature of the ground is exchanged for the warm air that penetrates the pipe. Along a hundred-foot pipe, the surrounding soil heats up and brings down the temperature in the air through the simple physics of heat exchange.

The result is a comfortable flow of cool air entering your home without the help of fossil fuel-dependent chemicals, compressors, or central cooling systems. As a general rule of thumb, the lower the average surface temperature, the fewer tubes you need. Due to the low underground temperature, you can also avoid overfilling the pipes. In most cold climates, a depth of two feet should be more than enough to reach the optimum soil temperature to cool the house.

STEP 4: MAPPING

Once you've carefully observed your land, you're ready to begin the process of mapping out your permaculture site. Mapping is important, whether you're developing a full-fledged forty-acre farm, a backyard plot, or an inner-city rooftop garden. The practice of mapping will allow you to conscientiously take into consideration all the different elements you encountered during the process of observation and design accordingly. There are several types of maps that you can draw. We're going to talk about four such maps in this section, and help you choose the best option.

Slope/Topographic Map (Step 4.1)

First off, you don't need to have a detailed topographical map like the maps used for hiking. It is entirely possible to discover the slope of your land through observation. Walking over your land will help you find where the land slopes and where it is level. Watching how rainwater runs will also alert you about the subtle shifts in slope.

Building an A-frame (explained in Chapter 4) is a fantastic way to discover the contours of your land without relying on expensive equipment. A water level can be built in an hour, and with the help of some stakes and a few friends, you can discover the contour of your whole land in a day.

Having a topographic or slope map will help you to consider where to place certain infrastructure on your land. For example, you wouldn't want to put a barn in an area where water will accumulate. It will also help you plan what would be the best way to plant an orchard. If you want to plant some fruit trees on a hillside, planting them on a contour will help improve yield and stop soil erosion in the long run.

Water Map (Step 4.2)

Drawing a water map is an important and necessary step of permaculture design. Careful observation will help you take into account where water enters and exits your land, pinpoint the sources of water, and work out how water can be slowed, spread, absorbed, and in some cases, moved throughout the land.

Before beginning the process of drawing your water map, the following set of questions will help you consider some oft-forgotten aspects of water management:

- Where does water enter your land?

- Where does it exit your land?

- Where does water run over your land and cause erosion? What can you do to stop that erosion and where can the water sink into your land?

- Where would a good place be for a pond?

- Is it possible to store water on the highest possible part of your land to develop an irrigation and water system that is driven by gravity?

- Where could you build a water tank on your land?

- What will you do with the rainwater falling on your roof? Can you store it or use it in some other way?

- What about the greywater from your showers and sinks? Can you reuse it in some way?

- Is it possible to build swales on your land to help store water?

- Is it possible to move water from one storage tank/pond to another storage tank/pond?

Pondering over the elements in these questions will help you to find the best way to use water to your advantage on your land. Make notes, and select all the options you can implement. If you have long-term plans, like solving the rainwater storage or greywater recycling, set up a priority list and keep it in mind when you're mapping out the whole project.

Zone and Sector Map (Step 4.3)

A zone and sector analysis will help you determine what parts of your land are best suited for different purposes. Once you've determined the zones on your land, you can map out what you plan to grow or do in each zone. For example, if you plan on planting a garden in zone 2 of your land (close to your house), but find yourself dealing with strong northern winds that will affect that garden, then you may want to plant a windbreak hedge. This way you can protect your garden from the wind while at the same time creating a heat trap for the southern sun, which promotes fruiting. The figure below illustrates how a wind break works.

Frequent wind direction

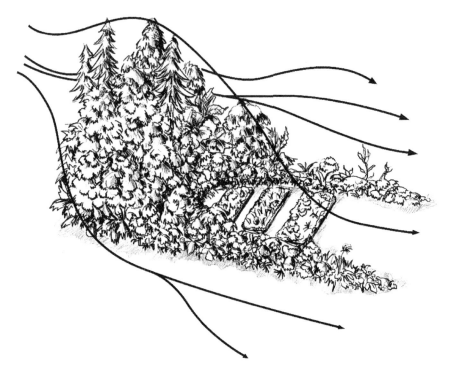

Figure 3.2: A windbreak hedge blocking strong gusts of wind.

Mapping in Practice – New Tools Available (Step 4.4)

Reading the above steps may have you wondering how you could achieve all this in practice. Although permaculture is first and foremost a way to put people in direct contact with the land, technology can play a helpful role, especially during the process of designing and mapping out your land.

If you have a smartphone, you can download different apps to map elevation. Taking a walk around your site or between the high point and low point can help you map elevation changes that you'll need to take into account. This can help you discover the distance and elevation change between a low point on your land where a small river passes and the high point on the land where you may want to build a water storage tank.

Google Earth is a free online program that can give you fairly clear aerial views of your land and can even be used to give "street views" of how your site will look from different parts of the land. You can print a map of your property as well by using Google Maps. Print it and trace the outline on a white sheet of paper by placing it over the print out. You can proceed to design your permaculture garden on this landscape map.

Play around with where you want different things and try different variations, then settle on the best one. This can be a perfect solution as a base for your garden design.

Furthermore, there are dozens of quality plant databases on the web that offer loads of information on the specific needs and characteristics of thousands of plants. These databases can help you find useful exotic species that might find a good niche on your site.

The Apios Institute has an edible forest garden wiki-like research database for the perennial-loving community to collaborate on (www.apiosinstitute.org). Plants for a Future (www.pfaf.org) offers information on over 7,000 different types of plants and their unique uses. Knowing how to use modern technology to your advantage can help you immensely during the design process.

STEP 5: CHOOSE THE RIGHT PLANTS

Once you have a fairly in-depth understanding of the slope, the water, and the zones and sectors of your land, you're ready to start thinking about what you want to plant (or build) and where. The final design map for your site should include a fairly detailed description of where you want your house, greenhouse, barn, and other infrastructure; where you'll plant a small forest or orchard; where your vegetable garden will be; where you plan to pasture animals if you have any; where your garden will be; and where you'll maintain any wild areas.

Though it's not necessary to include every minute detail like every single tomato plant, it is helpful to be as detailed as possible. Some design elements of your final map may change as you spend more time on your land and develop a thorough understanding of its specific conditions, but it is helpful to know what you plan to grow, where you want to plant it, and why.

Permaculture focuses on a plant's yield, characteristics, and functions within the design. So the characteristics of citrus trees could include that they're evergreen, have aromatic flowers and leaves, and give fruit. In a permaculture garden, they could function as a windbreak and a part of a suntrap. Moreover, citrus trees yield several useful products such as fruits, juice, jam, seeds, peel, aromatic oils, and timber.

Knowing the characteristics, yield, and function of different plants can help you decide the best place for growing them. If you want to plant trees to create a windbreak then you need to look for plants that are evergreens, anchored deep into the ground, have small leaves, are multi-stemmed, and bun-shaped such as Italian alder, sea buckthorn and small leaved lime.

Choose Plants from Important Food Groups

Plants belonging to the same family prefer the same growing conditions. So if you've figured out the growing conditions for one member, then you can easily work out the preferred conditions for the other members. For example, cabbages grow best in cooler conditions and are heavy feeders, so they require rich soil. Tomatoes, if they're grown in the northern hemisphere, tend to be summer crops (they grow best during winters if grown in the hot tropics). When you know the preferred growing conditions of each plant, you know when to plant different crops so that you can fulfill your food requirements throughout the year.

Two of the most important plant families are the legume family and the cereal family. Plants belonging to the legume family live in symbiosis with nitrogen-fixing bacteria. These bacteria cling to the roots, providing soluble nitrogen to the plants and adding nitrogen to the rhizosphere i.e., the area around the roots. These plants supply nutrients to the soil and are an essential part of our diet. Cereal plants are called staple crops because they're packed with energy and carbohydrates and make up a large part of our diet. Other important food groups include melons, onions, tomatoes, and root crops such as turnips, carrots, parsnips, radishes, and potatoes.

Planning the Garden Layout

Keep the wind and sun patterns in mind before you start designing the base layout of your permaculture garden. The microclimate on your site, type of soil, and water plans should be considered while planning your garden's layout. Here are some ideas to help you while mapping out your permaculture site.

Start with small structures, such as a small vegetable garden, so that you can figure out and correct any mistakes before moving on to the next stage. Focus on permanent structures. Decide their locations after taking into consideration the knowledge that you've gained about the different environmental factors through keen observation and careful thought. If you run out of budget for setting up large infrastructures, you can set them up later. Mark the space where you want them and only use it for short-term activities. Some examples of permanent structures include a garden shed, herb spiral, clothesline, cold frames, hotbeds, water tanks, keyhole beds, fixed animal housing, pergolas, and trellises.

Design circular, spiral, or winding paths so that you accomplish more than one thing during a single walk across your site. For example, a winding path might see you feeding the hens, collecting eggs, hanging the clothes, and visiting the cold frames. Don't waste space on small, fussy lawns. Place structures for related activities close together. For example, group a potting shed and greenhouse together, place a worm farm close to the vegetable garden with the compost bin in the center.

In the figure given below, you can see an herb spiral with rosemary growing in the center and other herbs such as thyme, chives, and chamomile growing in a spiral around it. Because rosemary prefers well-drained soil, it's a good idea to place it in the center where the soil is high enough to drain properly. Dill prefers soil that is consistently moist and a spot that receives the morning sun. It can tolerate afternoon shade and grows to a considerable size, so it's best to plant this along the spiral in a place where it wouldn't block sunlight for other plants.

Chives grow best under the full sun but can tolerate some shade, so place them midway through the spiral on the east or the west side. Thyme enjoys shade and sandy soil, so place it near rosemary. Mint grows best in soil that is constantly wet, so its ideal spot in the herbal spiral is near the watercress.

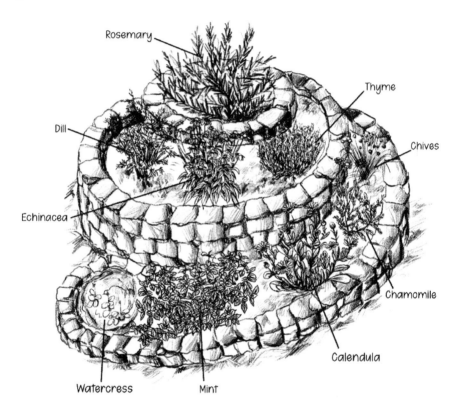

Figure 3.3: Herbal spiral.

Planning Where to Plant

Deciding where to plant depends on a number of different factors such as how frequently you'll be harvesting the plant, the level of maintenance that it requires, the plant's requirements and its shape, and how much space it will take up when it matures to full size. Here are some places that you can utilize for planting different crops:

1. **The Kitchen Door**

   Citrus trees such as lemon and lime can be planted near the kitchen door with a small herb garden underneath. Choose those varieties that harvest once or twice a year, such as chives or parsley.

2. **Herb Spiral**

   Medicinal and culinary herbs could be grown on the other side of the kitchen door such as thyme, oregano, basil, and sage. A spiral formation allows you to create different microclimates so that you can grow a wide variety of plants suited to different conditions. It's a good idea to plant a combination of annual and perennial herbs.

3. **Clipping Beds**

   Perennial plants that are clipped for their edible leaves, such as corn salads, chives, dandelions, mustard greens, and sorrels, can be planted along the edge of the winding or spiral path. Placing them near the path protects them against the wind, gives them access to plenty of sunlight, and makes it easy to perform frequent clippings.

4. **Plucking Beds**

   Fast-growing, tall plants can be planted behind the clipping beds, near the house. These plants include broccoli, kale, Swiss chard, silverbeet, English spinach, Brussels sprouts, celery, and coriander.

5. **Narrow Beds**

   Plants that grow vertically and require lots of sunlight can be planted beside the plucking beds. These beds are aligned from north to south and receive morning and afternoon sun. Some plants that can be grown in narrow beds include okra, eggplants, tomatoes, radishes, climbing peas, beans, carrots, and asparagus.

6. **Broad Beds**

   Plants that are low maintenance and slow growers can be planted behind the narrow beds. These include pumpkin, sugarcanes, cauliflower, cabbages, and lupins. Jerusalem and globe artichokes can be used as temporary windbreaks and suntraps.

7. **Broad-Scale Beds**

   These include staple foods such as grains that can be grown through alley cropping or the Fukuoka method, which involves building healthy growing systems by working in harmony with nature. Corn, wheat, barley, millet, sorghum, rice, and potatoes are some high-yielding plants to choose from.

8. **Trellis Crops**

   You can utilize fences, pergolas, and the sides of buildings to grow climbing plants such as peas, beans, passionfruit, kiwifruit, brambles, grapes, snake gourds and cucumbers.

STEP 6: OPTIMIZE YOUR GARDEN

If you want to include a particular plant or building on your site but you can't seem to find the right conditions for it to grow or you can't find the space for the building, then it's best to drop the idea. Permaculture is all about going with the flow and allowing nature to do the work. If something doesn't fit in your permaculture garden, then it's best not to force it into your garden layout.

STEP 7: LEARN, ADAPT, AND NEVER HESITATE TO CHANGE

Designing a map for your permaculture site can help you circumvent future problems and make the most of your land; however, it should not limit or restrict you from making changes as you gain more insight and knowledge about your site. As you finish building the permaculture garden that you've designed and begin living on your land, you might notice some of your plans fall through. Retain those aspects of your design that work and discard those that don't. Keep changing, adapting, and growing as you go along. Optimize your permaculture design by taking out the things that don't work and replacing them with things that do.

Action Plan for Designing Permaculture Garden

Here is a quick recap of everything that we've learned about permaculture design:

- Make observations and connect the dots. Notice how different elements work together and how you can harvest different energies to your benefit. For example, note which places on your land get the most sun and which don't get any, where the water flows naturally, which place has the highest abundance of animals, etc.

- Make a list of the plants that you want to grow and match them with different microclimates on your land.

- Sketch a base layout for your garden and make sure to draw each tree exactly where you want it.

- Group similar structures together to ensure ease of access and an easy workflow.

- The final map for your permaculture garden is not set in stone and you can make changes as you learn more. Keep optimizing, correcting, and improving your design as you go along, which is exactly what nature does.

CHAPTER 4

The Fundamental Importance of Soil and Water Stewardship

"The soil is the great connector of life, the source and destination of all. It is the healer and restorer and resurrector, by which disease passes into health, ages into youth, death into life. Without proper care for it, we can have no community because without proper care for it we can have no life."

— Wendell Berry,
The Unsettling of America: Culture and Agriculture

When humanity lived close to nature, the soil was cared for and replenished by farmers who understood that without the fertile topsoil, they wouldn't have anything to eat.

According to the United Nations, soil is a non-renewable resource, because it's not possible to recover its loss and degradation within the human lifespan. That's not good news for people aiming at sustainable living. Over a third of our Earth's land may be unable to naturally produce the nutrients that we require. What makes matters worse is that the land lost due to soil erosion cannot be recovered in our lifetime.

We live on a planet that is overflowing with life. If you've ever had to deal with a bumper crop of zucchini or garlic or tomatoes, you may have experienced that sense of wonder at how much nature has to offer for free. However, the abundance of food depends entirely on a thin layer of fertile soil that covers certain parts of our world.

The poet and farmer Wendell Berry once advised humans to "put your faith in the two inches of humus that will build underneath the trees every thousand years." When that's gone, our world may very well look more like Mars.

Soil Conservation Techniques

Some of you may be thinking right now: "Okay, you convinced me. We can't continue to lose the precious topsoil, but we don't exactly have 1,000 years to just let the soil naturally replenish itself. Are we doomed?"

Well, one of the most important concepts in permaculture is that of *accelerated succession.* In the case of topsoil, the accelerated succession would have us looking for ways to help the soil rebuild its natural fertility in less than a thousand years. Natural systems always tend to evolve towards holistic health and fertility.

Permaculture means trusting nature and allowing it to heal on its own; however, it also equips us with certain techniques that can help speed up the process of recovery. In the case of topsoil, there are a number of techniques, methods of cultivation, and production systems that we can employ to help the land regain its vigor and become fertile again. As we'll see below, in some cases, the two inches of topsoil that nature would generate in 1,000 years can be made in as few as four years.

Mulch

Look around you and you'll notice the ground under your feet showing signs of life, even when it is left to its own devices. Whether it's invasive grasses, weeds, diverse prairie, or the fallen leaves from an old tree, it is clear that nature wants the earth covered with something.

Mulch is often thought of as the chemically colored wood chips that are used for decorating the landscape in suburban America. Mulch, however, is any material that you can spread over the bare earth around whatever you are growing. We are most interested in dead, organic material that will eventually break down into the soil and enrich it. The art of mulching is the practice of learning from trees and how they naturally function. The leaves that fall on the forest floor are nature's mulch. The benefits of mulching the land we cultivate are many, but mainly it protects the soil from the harsh rays of the scorching sun, helping it retain moisture much longer.

In response to climate change, many farmers have begun to mulch their fields immediately after planting using old corn stalks, leaf litter, and even semi-composted sawdust from nearby sawmills. As a result of mulching, the soil can retain moisture, allowing the plants to grow, even if it doesn't rain that much.

Mulching the ground with organic matter also adds essential nutrients to the soil. As the mulch decomposes, it eventually turns into fertile black topsoil, replenishing lost nutrients. Mulching also allows soil life to flourish. It's important to note that tilling and exposing the earth to the sun, rain and other elements is genocide for the billions of unseen soil organisms, whereas maintaining a thick layer of mulch allows that soil food web (discussed below) to flourish.

Mulch can come from any number of sources. If you don't have a large area of land, purchasing a couple of hay bales or straw bales from a local farmer will give you more than enough organic material to keep your soil well protected and covered. Instead of burning the leaves that fall during autumn, use them as mulch for your garden beds in the winter. Pretty much any source of organic material will do, and with mulching, the more the better.

Ruth Stout, a steadfast organic farmer, developed an excellent gardening system based on an excessive amount of mulch. Speaking about her system, she says: "My no-work gardening method is simply to keep a thick mulch of any vegetable matter that rots on both my vegetable and flower garden all year round. As it decays and enriches the soil, I add more. The labor-saving part of my system is that I never plow, spade, sow a cover crop, harrow, hoe, cultivate, weed, water, or spray. I use just one fertilizer (cottonseed or soybean meal), and I don't go through that tortuous business of building a compost pile. I beg everyone to start with a mulch eight inches deep; otherwise, weeds may come through, and it would be a pity to be discouraged at the very start."

Another method, popularized by Charles Dowding, uses layers of cardboard covered in rotted organic matter. The cardboard layer is especially effective at suppressing weeds because it excludes all light and forms a barrier that is harder for their shoots to penetrate. The cardboard means that you need less mulch than you otherwise would, which in my experience is really helpful, as laying 8" of mulch requires an awful lot of mulch material!

If you live in an urban area, another excellent source of mulch is wood chips. Electrical companies usually produce truckloads of wood chips from the trees they trim around power lines, and many times they will willingly drop off a truckload of wood chips at your place if you offer to pay a small delivery fee.

If you are having a hard time finding organic material for mulch, you can simply grow your own. A quarter acre of wheat, rye, buckwheat, alfalfa, or pretty much any grain or cover crop can be grown in a couple of months. Besides the food you reap, you can harvest the straw or hay (hay is a crop that is grown as animal feed while straw is the byproduct of grains such as wheat, rye and barley) to be used as mulch on other parts of your land.

LASAGNA MULCH

Paper and cardboard are also organic materials that can be used as mulch. They come with an added benefit since they are thick (especially cardboard) so they can smother unwanted grass and other weeds below before eventually decomposing into the soil.

Lasagna gardening is a system of creating rich topsoil in a short amount of time without ever tilling the earth. The name comes from the layers of different mulch materials that you add one on top of the other to create a bed that will quickly decompose into rich topsoil. Essentially, you will be adding layers of organic materials that will decompose over time, resulting in rich, fluffy soil that will help your plants thrive.

To create your lasagna garden bed, you will need the following materials:

1. Cardboard or a large stack of newspapers
2. Straw or hay
3. A variety of "mulchable" materials such as:
   - Grass clippings
   - Leaves
   - Fruit and Vegetable Scraps
   - Coffee Grounds
   - Tea leaves and tea bags
   - Manure
   - Seaweed
   - Shredded newspaper or junk mail
   - Pine needles

The more diverse materials you use, the richer your soil will be. To make your lasagna garden bed, first, mow the area where you plan to make the bed. Add a layer of manure that will add nutrients and help speed up the decomposition of the cardboard. Next, lay the cardboard or newspaper on the ground to smother the grasses or weeds below.

On top of the cardboard, spread a layer of straw or hay mixed with other mulch materials that you have on hand. As Ruth Stout recommends, pile up your lasagna mulch, making it at least eight inches thick (the thicker the better). Save a bit of straw or hay for the final layer.

You can plant immediately in your lasagna garden bed, and the soil will only improve over time. To maintain soil fertility, you will have to continue adding "layers" each year.

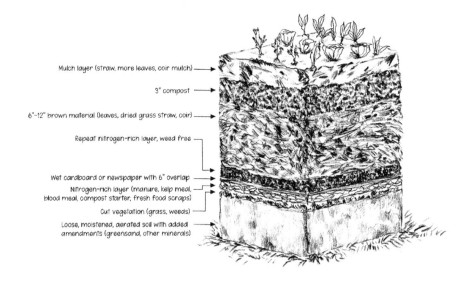

Mulch layer (straw, more leaves, coir mulch)

3" compost

6"-12" brown material (leaves, dried grass straw, coir)

Repeat nitrogen-rich layer, weed free

Wet cardboard or newspaper with 6" overlap

Nitrogen-rich layer (manure, kelp meal, blood meal, compost starter, fresh food scraps)

Cut vegetation (grass, weeds)

Loose, moistened, aerated soil with added amendments (greensand, other minerals)

Figure 4.1: Lasagna garden bed.

COVER CROPS

If you're trying to grow a permaculture garden in a small backyard, then mulching through a raised bed system or with lasagna gardening is probably the most efficient way to build and protect the soil. If, however, you have a little bit more land, finding enough mulch to cover an acre can be quite a challenge.

Cover crops are crops that are grown for their effect on soil fertility or as livestock fodder. They usually aren't grown as a food product, though it is possible to harvest small amounts of food from your cover crop. Since regular crops do pull nutrients from the soil, it is necessary to find a way to return those nutrients to the soil in a natural way.

Cover crops are grown in between growing periods as a way to cover the soil, add organic matter, and add nutrients to the soil that the other crops use up. In essence, cover crops are like "living mulch" that you grow. Cover crops improve the stability of soil while also adding biodiversity to your land. Other benefits of cover crops include:

- They protect the soil during fallow periods
- They aid in the mobilization and recycling of nutrients needed by plants
- They improve the soil structure and can help loosen the soil
- They permit healthy crop rotation (instead of monoculture)
- They can be used to control weeds and pests

Alfalfa is a great cover crop that can be grown in a variety of climates and soil types. It is a legume, meaning that it has the ability to trap nitrogen from the air and deposit it in the soil. Alfalfa also adds large amounts of organic matter to the soil and can also be used as fodder for the animals that you may keep. If your soil is nitrogen deficient (i.e., if your plant leaves are turning yellow), adding a cover crop of alfalfa once a year will greatly improve the nitrogen content in the soil.

Other quality cover crops and their benefits are as follows:
- Rye (Abundant organic matter)
- Hairy Vetch (Adds nitrogen and biomass)
- Oats (Can be used as animal fodder or a marketable food product)
- Peas (Adds nitrogen and can also be eaten)
- Wheat (Great for no-till systems and can be eaten)

- Daikon Radish (The large tuber helps to break up hardpan soils)

GREEN MANURES

Green manures are the same as cover crops. We use the term cover crop when the plant is alive while the term green manure is used when the plants have been cut and are decaying as mulch.

While many large-scale farmers will till their green manures, this practice also has risks. While the soil does benefit from the nutrients that are tilled into the soil, the upturned soil gets exposed to the effects of erosion. Furthermore, tilling disrupts the work of soil organisms.

Simply allowing the green manure to naturally decompose on the soil is the best way to take advantage of the benefits to the soil that it creates. Many times people will cut down the green manure before it goes to seed. This helps prevent the green manure/cover crop from reseeding itself. Moreover, since plants use large amounts of energy and nutrients in the process of producing seeds, chopping down the cover crop right when flowering begins is the best way to get the most nutrients from your green manure.

For people who want to replenish the soil on large tracts of land, using green manure is a much more manageable and cheaper way than hauling in truckloads of compost or adding a thick layer of mulch over the entire land. Furthermore, if you have a problem with some sort of invasive weed, heavy green manure with buckwheat or other crops that produce abundant organic material can out-compete the weeds.

Lastly, certain green manures can even be used as a living mulch while you're growing your marketable/edible crops. White clover forms a dense carpet over the soil while not growing taller than a couple of inches. It doesn't spread over other crops, suffocating them and cutting out their nutrient supply, and also adds nitrogen to the soil.

The Importance of Contour

The last technique for soil conservation that we will look at is working with the contours of your land. Contour is nothing more than level lines. By finding contours on the slopes, you can create different types of "buffers" that help to prevent erosion.

If the sloped land is not properly covered, the topsoil will most likely erode during the rainy season. In places like Iowa, which is not too hilly, the topsoil loss we discussed earlier is mostly due to the rain falling on bare soil and running off the land.

To find contour lines on your land, there are a number of simple instruments that you can make at home. The simplest tool for finding the level of the land is an A-frame level (see below for instructions). With this tool, you can quickly and easily mark the contour lines on your land with a series of posts or stakes.

The easiest way to stop erosion is to simply pile up organic material along the contour lines on the slope. Old corn stalks, the brush pile behind your house, a fallen tree, or anything else can be used to stop the soil from washing away. Alternatively, you can plant deep-rooted grasses such as vetiver (khus) grass along the contour line. These grasses form a wall that will stop the soil washing away with the rain. Over time, as the soil builds up along the contour lines, your land will begin to resemble a series of curved terraces, reminiscent of the terraced rice fields of Asia.

Planting trees or bushes on the contour is another way to form a permanent barrier that will help stop erosion in the long run. The trees or bushes planted in rows will also provide organic material for mulching your soil in between the contour lines.

BUILD YOUR OWN A-FRAME LEVEL

To build your A-frame level you will need:
- Two pieces of wood 1.5 meters long (60")
- One piece of wood 1 meter long (40")

- Nails and a hammer

- A piece of string

- A rock or plumb bob

To make the A-frame level, simply nail together the two pieces of two-meter long wood for the "legs" then nail the one-meter piece of wood near the middle to form the letter A. Tie a piece of string to a nail placed at the top of the "A" and let the string hang below the horizontal piece of the 1-meter wood. Tie a rock or connect the plumb bob to the end of the piece of string.

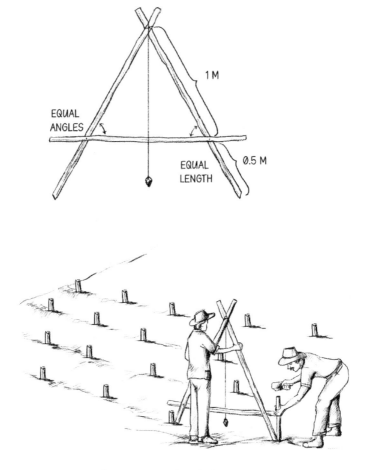

Figure 4.2: An A-Frame.

To calibrate the A-frame level, place the two legs on the ground and mark the place where each leg sits. Let the string dangle and when it stops moving, simply place a mark along with the horizontal piece of wood where the string touches. Next, change the position of the legs so that each leg is resting in the same place that the opposite leg was. Your string should now dangle on the opposite side of the horizontal piece of wood. When it stops moving, make another mark. The midpoint between those two marks is your level. Use a ruler or tape measure to find the exact middle between the two marks and use a small stake to make another, more permanent mark.

To find the contour of your land, take the A-frame level and place it horizontally along a slope. Keep one leg still and move the other leg until the string falls directly on your middle mark. Place two stakes where the legs of the A-frame level are. Then move the A-frame level to the end of one of the stakes and continue to find the next level. You should end up with a row of stakes that snake or curve across your land showing you the contour of your slope.

The Compost Pile

The compost pile is a truly ingenious idea that allows you to utilize household and gardening waste to grow plants. Food scraps from the kitchen, fallen leaves, grass clippings, and even dog poop can be turned into rich, fertile soil. The process of making compost is fairly simple and involves providing the right conditions to promote the growth of microorganisms. There is no recipe for creating compost; however, there are a few guidelines that you need to follow:

1. The more variety you add to your compost the better. Simply adding chicken manure or wheat straw would not give your compost a decent amount of nutrient content.

2. Understanding the "browns-to-greens ratio" is necessary for creating a compost pile. The "greens" refers to dead but not decaying materials such as recently cut vegetable and fruit

scraps, fresh grass clippings, and manure. They are mostly nitrogen based. The "browns" are older, long dead materials that are carbon based, such as wood chips, twigs and straw. Too much carbon will slow your pile's decomposition, too much nitrogen is likely to cause your pile to smell bad (rule of thumb: if your compost stinks, add carbon)

3. In terms of weight, a carbon: nitrogen ratio of 25:1 is usually the best. If you don't want to weigh everything, you can start with 50:50 by volume and adjust from there.

4. Add nitrogen-fixing tree material such as leaves from nitrogen-fixing trees such as black locust and alder trees.

5. Don't cut off the air completely. The biggest mistake that people make with their compost pile is that they cut off oxygen completely to promote the growth of anaerobic microbes. Here's a general rule of thumb: your compost should never smell bad. Keep it aerated. If it starts giving off a pungent smell, turn it over and let it get some fresh air.

6. Water regularly but avoid adding too much. An excessive amount of water can generate anaerobic conditions.

7. Turn the compost over often to speed up the action of microorganisms. Most people turn their compost piles every four or five weeks. If you turn your compost pile more often (every two or three weeks), the compost will be made faster. To promote maximum bacterial activity, wait a minimum of two weeks between turns. This time is enough to allow the center of the pile to heat up. In summer, you can turn the compost more often, as composting happens more quickly in the heat.

8. The compost is ready when it turns black and gives off an earthy rainy smell.

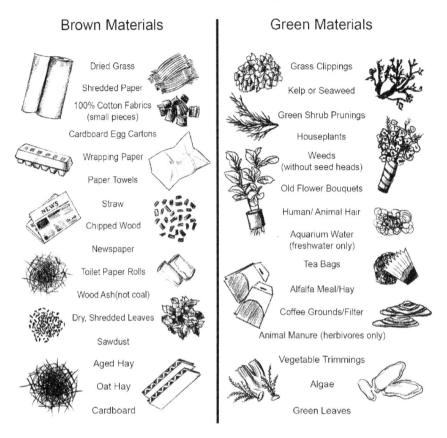

Figure 4.3: Different sources for making compost.

What not to compost?

There are some materials that you should add only in small amounts to your compost bin. These include onion scraps, citrus peels, egg shells, and stale bread. However, there are also some items that you should never put in your compost bin – except if you are an expert.

- Dairy, fats, oils, bones, meat and fish leftovers
- Dog, cat or human waste, diapers

- Manure from sick animals
- Plants or wood treated with chemicals (pesticides or preservatives)
- Insect-infested, diseased and naturally toxic plants (like black walnut)
- Weeds that already developed seeds
- Glossy or color-printed paper, magazines, coated cardboard

Most of these can be composted only with a proper "hot compost" system. Adding a dead animal is often used as a concentrated Nitrogen pocket to kick-start the process (Comfrey can also be used) – but I suggest avoiding this in your small-scale garden.

Worm Farming

Worms are known as nature's soil makers. They burrow tunnels in the soil, breaking it down, eating up organic matter, and making the soil more fertile by producing worm castings. Worm farming is an excellent way to transform food waste into fertilizer. California red worms or Red Wigglers are a great choice for worm farming as they don't grow too large and they reproduce quickly. Follow the steps outlined below to make your own worm farm:

1. **Step 1:**
   You can build a worm farm with any old, large container (I used an opaque, ten-gallon, plastic storage tub). Take a sharp, pointed object and poke a few small holes at the bottom of the container as well as the sides. The holes at the bottom will allow drainage while the ones on the sides are for ventilation.

2. **Step 2:**
   Line the bottom of the container with shredded newspaper. Use a water spray bottle to mist the paper to make it damp but not too wet. Worms thrive in a slightly moist environment.

3. **Step 3:**

Add some food scraps such as coffee grounds, vegetable and fruit peels, and leaves then line with shredded newspaper. Add another layer of scraps and finish off with a final layer of shredded paper. Fill three quarters of the container and make sure to avoid meat or oil, which can attract flies and maggots.

4. **Step 4:**

Toss your worms into the bin. The worms quickly devour kitchen scraps, turning them into rich, dark humus. Moreover, you can harvest worm castings by simply adding the feed on one side of the container. The worms slowly move toward the food, leaving behind castings that can easily be picked up.

5. **Step 5:**

Keep the worm bin somewhere warm. A heated garage, laundry room or basement are ideal locations. The worms perform their best at temperatures between 59°F and 77°F $(15 - 25 \text{ C}^\circ)$.

6. **Step 6:**

Feed the worms kitchen scraps after every few days by digging a hole with a hand trowel and burying the kitchen waste inside. Some form of grit is also important (ground eggshells is a common option). Put the food in a different place each time. If the worm bin looks too soggy or gives off a foul smell (which it should not) then add some dry bedding (shredded paper) to soak up the moisture.

7. **Step 7:**

Your worm compost should have a dark color, give off an earthy smell and crumble in your hand when it's ready. Sift the worms, placing them back in the bin, and add the compost to your plants.

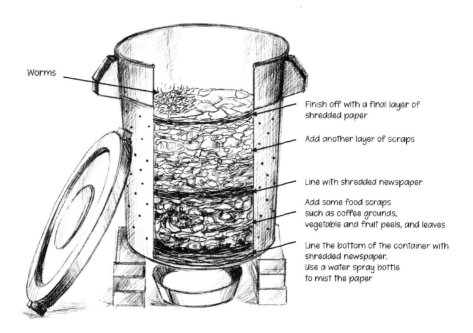

Worms

Finish off with a final layer of shredded paper

Add another layer of scraps

Line with shredded newspaper

Add some food scraps such as coffee grounds, vegetable and fruit peels, and leaves

Line the bottom of the container with shredded newspaper. Use a water spray bottle to mist the paper

Figure 4.4: Worm Compost Bin

However if you like DIY, you can easily create something very pretty from simple wood boxes. The "worm-hive" is a multi-layer farm, which is a somewhat more sophisticated model. The method is the same, but it's much more visually appealing than the plastic storage tubs or buckets.

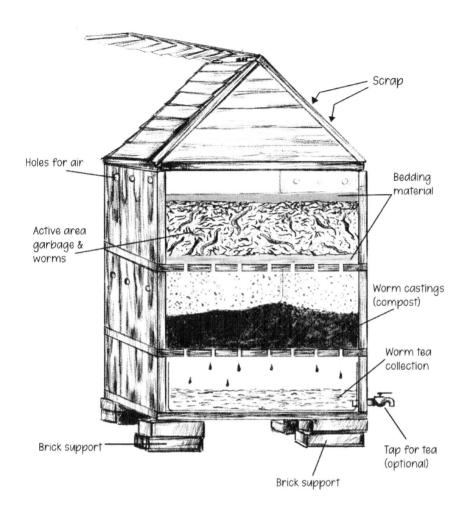

Figure 4.5: Worm Hive

Compost Tea

There's nothing more refreshing than sipping a cup of tea on a balmy afternoon, and just like you, your plants may be craving for a cup or two of freshly brewed tea of a slightly different kind.

Compost tea is a blend of organic matter that has been produced to boost soil fertility. It is a liquid that is extracted by beneficial microorganisms through a process called brewing. Most processes of making compost tea are a bit complex, so making store-bought compost tea powders is a good option. If you still want to give homemade compost tea a go, then you can try the following process:

1. Mix a large handful of compost; a handful of garden soil; a handful of straw; and three to five leaves from a robust, healthy plant.
2. Put the mixture in a bag, tie it tightly and dip it into a bucket of water.
3. Pour 1 cup of seaweed extract and 1 cup of fish hydrolysate into the water.
4. Put an aerator in the bucket and turn it on.
5. Maintaining a temperature of 68 to 72 degrees Fahrenheit, (20-22 C°) brew the tea for approximately 36 hours.
6. Once your tea is ready, add three parts tea to one part water and spray on the plants in the morning or late in the afternoon.

If you find this method too complicated, you can also make comfrey or nettle tea by filling a bin with cut material, topping up with water and leaving it for a month or so to rot down. Simply dilute the black liquid that ensues and use it as a feed. Your plants will be happy.

Harvesting the Sun: Making the Most of Sunlight

Look up in the sky during the day and what do you see? It is impossible to ignore the blazing sun and its majestic beauty as it shines above and breathes life into our planet. Without it, the Earth would be a barren, desolate rock covered in ice, floating through space shrouded in darkness.

Even though the sun is the most prominent feature of the sky during the day, very few of us stop to think about charting its course and understanding how it changes its position throughout the day and during different seasons.

The side of the house or hill that faces the east or the west is known as sun facing, while those sides that point towards north and south are pole facing. The east-facing side receives the morning sun, which is great for melting frost that may have accumulated on the plants overnight. The west-facing side tends to be the hottest, because it receives harsh sunlight in the afternoon. (In some areas, like in Ontario, Canada, the south face is often the warmest year round because the sun is low enough that it hits the south face from sunrise to sunset.) The pole-facing sides of the house or hill will be the coolest regions which will remain shaded for most of the day during winters.

The Importance of Water: Water Management

It is inconceivable to grow anything without water, but while water is essential for growing plants, agricultural runoff leads to soil erosion, and changing the path of water for irrigation depletes natural aquifers. Here are some ways that we can help to prevent the loss of soil fertility and make the most of our water resources.

SLOW IT, SPREAD IT, SINK IT: PERMACULTURE'S TAKE ON WHAT TO DO WITH WATER

Although soil conservation and "construction" are vital to any permaculture design, managing water is equally essential. Soil and water are intimately connected, and many of the processes for conserving soil will also conserve water.

So what can we do to try and preserve the increasingly scarce water resources? Climate change will continue to cause uncertainty in weather patterns that will disrupt farming traditions. While we may not be able to make it rain, we can make better use of the water that does fall. And since we are expecting to see an increase in heavy rains followed by longer periods of drought, we would do well to learn how to make the most of the water that does come our way.

Permaculture asserts that the best approach to effective water management is to "slow it, spread it, and sink it." We will look at each one of those facets individually.

Slow It

If you've ever been outside during a heavy rainstorm, you may have witnessed the full force of nature and the incredible destruction that water can cause. The land begins to absorb the moisture, especially if it has been dry. After a certain point, however, the soil becomes so saturated that the water begins to pool. If you are on any type of slope, the excess water will follow the path of least resistance as it begins to flow downward in rivulets that form into gullies that eventually wash out the land.

The force of the water also takes anything with it that happens to be on the surface of the land, from garbage to precious, uncovered topsoil. Erosion is caused by leaving the ground bare and exposed to harsh winds and rains.

Permaculture water management techniques focus first on slowing down the water. The faster the water gushes down the land, the more it carries with it. We will discuss a few different techniques to slow, spread, and sink water in a little while, but one way to slow the movement of water across the landscape is by building a series of on-contour trenches called swales. As water runs down the slopes after heavy rain, it will go over the indentations which can slow it down and gives you control of where the water goes next.

Spread It

Once we've slowed down the water, we can try to do something with it that will benefit our land. By slowing down rainwater runoff, we are able to spread that water over the landscape, which helps us avoid the excessive accumulation of water in some parts of the land and the lack of water in other parts of the land.

If you were to build a series of swales along a slope, the water would seep into the ground rather than collecting at a low spot or running off your land entirely. You can consider building one of the swales slightly off contour to move the water to a pond or reservoir. The swale would then basically become a drainage ditch that could move water to a dry portion of the land where it could spread. A swale on contour with a level spillway or a couple swivel pipes can also allow you to decide where the water leaves the swale and at what water level.

SINK IT

As we spread water over our landscape, we also help it to sink into the ground. The best water management practices try to sink as much water into the ground as possible. So what are the benefits of letting water get absorbed by your land?

First, you need water to grow plants and soil is the best and most effective tool for storing water. While a couple of thousand dollars in investment may allow you to build a massive 100,000-gallon cement cistern, even a quarter acre of land could store ten times that much in the soil itself.

Furthermore, sinking water into the land helps replenish aquifers and other groundwater sources. In many cases, springs that have long gone dry from bad water management can be brought back to life once water is allowed to infiltrate into the ground.

Our swales then not only slow water and help to spread it over the landscape, but they also allow the water to sink into the land over time, thus helping to maintain the moisture in the land and allowing groundwater to recharge.

HOLDING WATER IN THE LAND

Slow it, spread it, and sink it: That is the essence of permaculture's take on water management. But what techniques can we use to effectively achieve this? There is no universal method that works for every piece of land. While a system of on-contour swales may do wonders at one place, a simple series of ponds may be more effective for other places.

INCREASE ORGANIC MATTER CONTENT

Our first (and most important) strategy for holding water in the land is to increase the organic matter content of the soil. Fertile, black topsoil with plentiful organic matter will hold much more water than earth that has eroded down to the clay-dominated subsoil. Humus, or rich topsoil, can hold 80-90% of its weight in water. If you have 100 pounds of topsoil, 80 to 90 pounds of water can be held by that soil.

One of the simplest ways to increase the organic matter in any soil is through mulching. If you have a small area of land to work with then you can add compost; however, larger areas may require the use of mulch. Leftover crop residues, which are often burned or discarded, can be left to decay on the land to provide a protective mulch for the next crop while also adding moisture to the topsoil.

CHECK DAMS

If a part of your land suffers from some sort of serious drainage problem caused by excessive run-off, check dams may help you slow the movement of water over land and increase its absorption by the soil. If a small ravine has formed from excessive, unchecked runoff, a swale won't be able an effective solution, as the water will continue to flow down the path it's carved in the ground, which offers the least resistance.

Check dams are simply a collection of rocks, debris, or other solid material that are placed along a ravine or creek bed. The purpose of a check dam is to slow the flow of water and to allow the water to build up behind the temporary dams during heavy rains. As a child, you probably made a few check dams without realizing it when you placed rocks, branches, and other debris near a small river to create a swimming pool for you and your friends.

The runoff which usually flows through the ravine, creek bed, or gully is momentarily backed up behind the dam. The silt, rocks, topsoil, and other material that the water carried deposits behind the dam gradually filled in the ravine to prevent erosion. The water that collects in the dam seeps into the soil, replenishing groundwater sources and often creating natural springs further downstream.

While check dams aren't recommended for areas where there is constant water flow (because of the potential damage that the dam could cause), they work remarkably well in areas where there is a small, seasonal water flow or areas where runoff concentrates during heavy and prolonged rainstorms.

One of the best ways to build check dams is with gabions. Gabions are an assortment of rocks that are assembled in wire mesh cages, giving them the appearance of large blocks of solid rock. They form a formidable barrier against strong currents and will usually last several lifetimes.

If you are looking for a less permanent option, simply gathering large rocks from the edge of a ravine and arranging them in a way that blocks the path of water is another acceptable option. Check dams can be constructed in different sizes depending on the intensity of the water flow. If only a small amount of water trickles as runoff on a slope on your land and you're worried that it might lead to erosion problems further down the road, a check dam of two to three layers of rock is usually enough.

Water-Saving Irrigation Practices

Storing water in the land is an easy and efficient way to manage the flow of water on your land. But what happens if you find yourself short of water for irrigation? The water underneath the soil will be near impossible to extract to fulfill your irrigation requirements. This is why you need to have multiple options for storing water that you can turn to in time of need.

Rainwater stored in large cisterns and tanks can be utilized when the water supply falls short through collecting it from roof guttering. This can be achieved by installing plain household gutters that transport water from the roof to a storage facility (large barrels or tanks). If you use open containers to store the water, I suggest placing a mosquito-net on top of the container. This will prevent insects falling into the water, and decrease the chance of other types of contamination as well.

Likewise, water from a nearby spring or river can be used to fulfill water requirements.

If we focus on saving and utilizing every single drop of water that we have, then we may never find ourselves in a position where we run out of water. Interestingly, the process of irrigation itself is an extremely wasteful practice, from traditional sprinkler systems to using helicopters and airplanes to spray water over a large portion of land that has nothing to do with growing crops.

However, drip irrigation is an excellent water-saving process that involves providing water to the root area of the plants only. By using drip irrigation, you can prevent up to 80% of water wastage. Moreover, targeting the root area prevents fungal diseases on the leaves caused by excessive moisture. Two kinds of drip irrigation systems that are extremely easy to set up include:

Bamboo Drip Irrigation

Bamboo plants can be grown easily all over the world except Antarctica and are highly water-resistant. Bamboo stems can be used as a building material or can be split and used as gutters for carrying rainwater. Drip irrigation can easily be achieved with bamboo of any size by splitting it into two halves with a machete and placing the bamboo along the rows of plants in your garden. Mark the place on the bamboo that is near a plant and drill small holes. Make sure to place the bamboo on a slight decline to ensure the flow of water. If the garden row is too long then you can join two or more pieces with glue or silicone to make sure the water reaches all the plants.

Bottle Irrigation

For small or container gardens, bottle irrigation is more feasible. Not only is it economical, but it also gets the job done efficiently. This is also a great technique to turn to if you're someone who forgets to water your plants or if you love traveling but don't want to kill your houseplants.

All you need for this method is a large plastic bottle (a two-liter soft drink bottle or a gallon milk jug will work fine). Heat a needle and pierce a small hole in the cap. Fill the bottle with water, close the cap and hang it over the plant. Tiny droplets of water will drip from the small hole onto your plant keeping the soil moist and satisfying the plant's watering needs even when you're away. If the water drips more than a few droplets per minute, then you could end up overwatering your plants. Another method involves inverting a bottle of water with a tiny hole in the bottle cap and sinking it into the soil, so it slowly empties out. There are also glass drip-waterers that perform the same function.

Waste Water Recycling

Water conservation is one of the most fundamental aspects of any permaculture design. Once we have designed and developed the practices and mechanisms to utilize the water on our land in the best possible ways, then we are ready to get started building our garden and growing food.

Reusing wastewater is one way to reap the maximum benefit of our water resources. Figuring out what works in our favor is the key to finding multiple uses for natural processes. We can see that plants and biologically active soil clean contaminated water in nature, so why don't we make use of these organisms to treat the gallons of wastewater that we generate each day?

Wastewater can be divided into two types: greywater, which is the slightly dirty water from sinks and showering, and blackwater, which is water from toilets. We can reuse both these types of water by including wetlands in our permaculture design. Compost toilets and reusing greywater are great options for people working with smaller set ups. Let's look at exactly what wetlands are and how we can make them.

WETLANDS

Wetlands are a crucial part of the natural ecosystem, but they're usually drained to erect tall buildings and housing projects. Wetlands are an excellent source of biodiversity. Introducing wetlands on your permaculture land allows you to store water and reuse greywater.

GREYWATER

Greywater is water from dishwashing, showering, and washing clothes. It has a high amount of phosphate from the soap residue, making it perfect for the growth of many plant species.

To create a wetland near your house, start by digging a hole in the ground approximately one meter deep. The exact size of the pond depends on the amount of water that you want it to hold and the kind of soil that is abundant on your land. Greywater gets soaked up by sandy soil, while thick clay soil doesn't absorb as much water. To avoid the water seeping into the ground, you can also line the base with a layer of cement, plastic or clay.

To make the water accumulate in the hole that you've dug, line the base with rocks, pumice stones, or gravel. Add water and water-purifying plant species such as cattails, calla lilies, and water reeds. Allow the plants to adjust to their new home for some time before redirecting the flow of greywater from your home to the pond. You can simply build the wetland below your house and let gravity do the work or you can redirect PVC pipes that leave your home by connecting them to a pumping system. Make sure that the plants cover the surface of the water so that the greywater comes into maximum contact with the plant's root systems and minimum contact with air. This will allow the microorganisms clinging to the elaborate root networks of the wetland plants to carry out the purification process.

If the soaps or detergents that you use contain strong chemicals, then you can filter them out by running the greywater through a simple filtration system. Take a small cinder block box, layer it with sand, gravel, and charcoal. Direct the greywater from your house to this filter and connect an exit hose at the bottom. Alternatively, you can install a commercial water filtration unit to treat wastewater or you can simply substitute harsh chemicals with mild, organic soaps and detergents.

BLACKWATER

To treat blackwater, you can make use of a system called an eco-machine or living machine. In this method, the wastewater flows through a series of tanks starting with a septic tank where solid residue settles at the bottom. (You may need additional chambers if you have enough people that you fill them too quickly.) A septic tank also provides the opportunity to collect biogas to fuel your kitchen. From here, the wastewater is pumped into an anaerobic tank, which helps digest more sediments. The water then goes into a highly aerobic environment in a tank that is filled with water-purifying plants.

Composting Toilets

Almost all conventional homes built today come with a plumbing system that is designed to take the waste that leaves our human bodies as far away as possible from us. "Out of sight and out of mind" is the rule of the game.

Permaculture, however, urges you to always recycle waste back into the system. From a sustainability standpoint, if we take from the land, we have an obligation to give back as well and there isn't any way more direct and tangible to give back to the earth than composting.

There are a number of different composting toilet designs. While commercially made composting toilets can be purchased, you can also build your own simple, double chamber composting toilet systems for a fairly low price. Human waste mostly has high nitrogen content. The right carbon to nitrogen content is crucial for making quality compost. We can transform both solid and liquid human waste into compost by mixing high nitrogen material such as sawdust, brown leaves, straw/hay, etc.

With a composting toilet, every time you use the bathroom, a scoop or two of sawdust, finely chopped straw, or other high carbon material is thrown into the toilet in place of the "flush." The double chamber composting toilet system comes with two different toilet seats with separate chambers. You use one of the chambers for several months until it fills up, then close it off, giving it time to sit and begin composting into humus. By the time the second chamber fills up, the waste that was in the first chamber will have composted down into dark, unscented soil.

You can use a shovel to get that compost out of the chamber (through an access door), pile it somewhere out of the way to continue to decompose for another six to twelve months, and you're ready to use the first chamber again.

The composting toilet system is about as close as you can get to universally appropriate technology to turn human waste into fertilizer without using up a ton of energy. Wherever you are in the world, nitrogen and carbon materials will pretty quickly decompose into a rich compost as long as you give them the needed conditions. Instead of wasting water on flush toilets that dump organic matter into a sewer system or bury them in a useless septic tank, composting toilets can help you save water while returning lost nutrients to the soil and making it more fertile.

In Chapter 5, we're going to discuss the methods and techniques required to grow delicious and healthy fruits and vegetables, free from harmful chemicals or genetic tweaking. We're going to look at ways that we can increase yields and how we can make the most of all the available resources to not only satisfy our needs but also increase profitability. We're also going to be looking at livestock and the important roles that animals can play on our land.

CHAPTER 5

Permaculture Tools
for Maximizing Yields

Now that we've learned about the ethics and principles of permaculture, the most essential tools for design, and the fundamental importance of preserving soil and water on our landscapes, we are ready to turn our attention to the issue of producing healthy, nourishing food for ourselves, our families, and our community. Let's take an in-depth look at several different strategies for creating an abundance of diverse food products, focusing both on perennial and annual strategies for food production. When we use the full scope of permaculture design tools, nature will provide us with an abundance of healthy food, fuel, fiber, and medicines for our wellbeing.

Food Forests and the Richness of Diversity

Imagine you go on a walk in the countryside. On one side of the road, you can see a golden field of wheat growing in neat rows stretching on for several acres. On the other side is an old forest full of tall trees and thick undergrowth. If someone asks you which side of the road produces the most food, you may feel tempted to choose the cornfields, because the forest, while extremely beautiful, is generally not considered productive.

We have been taught that food can only be grown in neat rows and that wild forests present a beautiful sight but simply cannot be a source of sustenance. Now imagine getting off the country road and walking into the old forest. Under the pine trees, you can see thousands of pine nuts on the ground. Oyster and shiitake mushrooms sprout from rotten stumps, and morels shoot up from a carpet of fallen leaves.

Wild forest blueberries provide fresh fruit outdoors, and gooseberries work well in the shade of large trees. You may also encounter old apple trees that are covered in fruits. Dense forests provide a great habitat for deer, turkeys, and other wildlife. Hundreds of other, lesser-known edible vegetables can be found growing on the forest floor.

We may not expect to find the same abundance of food that we'd find growing in neat little rows on the farm, but this belief couldn't be more wrong. The forests are bursting with a cornucopia of food from wild mushrooms to clusters of berries, and an abundance of wild animals for hunting. Forests are a source of food for wildlife and humans. We just have to train ourselves to look closer to find patterns that we might overlook at first glance.

Approach to Permaculture Diversity

Not all natural systems provide the same amount of food as the forest we just imagined. But through permaculture, we can observe the natural world and design landscapes that adhere to the principles of diversity and natural abundance. Having the ability to select which plants, trees, and animals live in our landscape, we can pick the best traits from natural ecosystems and build a food forest that fulfills all of our needs. For example, while some oaks provide edible acorns, we may prefer to replace them with chestnut and walnut trees. The undergrowth of ferns and other forest shrubs can be replaced with hazelnuts, gooseberries, and other edible crops.

Permaculture design principle number ten requires us to take advantage of and evaluate diversity. Cultivating different species not only mimics the way nature functions but also enhances resilience by creating an interactive and productive food system in which different species benefit from each other. Food forests are an opportunity to design edible landscapes that mimic the natural ecosystem of forests.

Livestock: The Role of Animals in Permaculture

Keeping livestock is a big decision that comes with a lot of responsibilities, so it's best not to take it lightly and buy a bunch of animals on a whim. It's a good idea to start small with a few young animals. Once you've reared them for quite some time, you can move on and increase your flock/herd or add additional species. It's important not to rush; instead grow and gain experience working with one kind of animal before moving on to the next.

CHICKENS

Chickens will scratch and peck at the soil looking for bugs, which is great to get rid of an excessive amount of worms in the soil (a large number of worms can destroy beneficial bacteria, fungi and eat up organic matter, reducing soil fertility), but too many chickens can cause more harm than good. While they are great for getting rid of unwanted bugs, they can sometimes cause root damage, consume all the earthworms required to keep soil healthy, and disturb mulched areas. So, what I like to do is use my chickens to clear unwanted pests from wooded areas. I simply let the chickens out of the pen and direct them to the area where I want to be cleared of insects (for example, a large population of ants) by using birdseed to lure them. This way I can put all the scratching and pecking to good use instead of having my herbs and vegetables destroyed. As the chickens feast on the insects, they're bound to leave some droppings behind, which is again beneficial for the tree's growth. Moreover, chickens are also useful for "tractoring" when areas of land need to be cleared of weeds for planting.

I like to keep my chickens next to my vegetable garden with a fence in between, so I can easily toss over food. I put leftover chicken feed and manure in the compost pile to make rich compost that can be used to fertilize fruit trees. The high nitrogen content of this compost can make it a bit too strong for vegetables and it may cause burning.

Figure 5.1: Chicken tractor design.

GEESE

You can use geese to manage the growth of wild plants in a food forest or permaculture garden. They are the only species of animals that only eat grasses and clovers, leaving other crops. A friend of mine who lives in Las Canadas in Huatusco, Mexico, used geese to get rid of a weedy star grass that would keep sprouting beneath his woody plants. He started with ten geese per acre; after a year he only needed two geese per acre to control the spread of grasses.

Now he has planted a multitude of different crops such as ginger, sweet potatoes, and taro, which could not be planted with star grass. The geese waddle through the crops, pecking at a few blades of grass sticking out of the ground here and there. My friend used the African weeder geese, although the same results could be achieved with most breeds.

DUCKS

The snails or slugs infesting your plants can be easily cleared by keeping a few ducks on your farm. They may nibble on the leaves a bit, so it's best to release only a few at a time to clear out an area. Indian runner ducks are particularly popular with permaculturists. They're good natured, hoover up slugs and snails, and are naturally flightless.

GOATS

Goats can be used in a manner similar to chickens to clear out unwanted weed plants such as lantana, privet, and camphor laurel. However, goats cannot reach the upper branches of a wild, or invasive tree or bush, so regular maintenance is required to clear out unwanted plant species from an area.

PIGS

Pigs are usually kept for their meat, but what a pig can do for you in your garden is truly amazing. They are great at tilling the land, especially if chickens follow after them. Pigs root naturally and find bugs, which saves labor as well as money! Pigs also fertilize the soil making it better than ever before. However, don't forget about fencing. It is a must-have for keeping the pigs inside the area you want them to dig and out of the places you don't.

SHEEP

Sheep grow wool, and provide meat and milk. Different breeds are suited to different climates. The sheep that live in hilly or mountainous regions tend to be more hardy than others and survive rough conditions. Lowland sheep require better pastures for grazing and shelter from harsh weather conditions. Sheep, along with chickens, can be used to clean brushes and wild grass and for tilling.

COWS

Cattle are divided into meat-producing breeds and milk-producing breeds. However, it's best to go for a breed that has both attributes. Dual-purpose breeds are a great option because cows need to have a calf to produce milk. Once the calf grows up, it can be used for providing beef. Moreover, cows play an essential role in maintaining biodiversity in the meadows and replenishing carbon content in the soil.

Integrating livestock into our permaculture design creates wonderful opportunities for us to put animals to good use and get work done. Like everything else about permaculture, this process requires close observation, thoughtful planning, and brainstorming ideas.

The Functions of a Tree

Orchards are fantastic. A well-maintained peach orchard will give you a steady crop for up to twenty years. An apple orchard can last up to fifty years and a well-maintained pecan tree may very well continue to produce nuts for up to 150 years.

Tree-based perennial farming systems offer many advantages over traditional annual farming methods. It will take several years to establish these systems, but the only work after production is maintenance and harvesting. Therefore, tree crops such as fruits and nuts can become an important part of our diet without tampering with the soil each year.

Permaculture requires us to find different functions for each element in our system. Trees are probably one of the most useful elements in permaculture design. Some of the features of the tree farming system are:

- Harvest: From fruits to nuts and edible leaves, there are many foods that trees can offer. Mushrooms growing symbiotically with living trees or feeding off of dead/dying trees and providing another yield after the tree's death.

- Mulch: The leaves of deciduous trees are one of the best mulch materials for farms and are important for improving the overall health of the soil. However, there are exceptions, such as black walnut, the leaves of which are highly toxic and can kill plants if used as mulch. Some plants like the Paw Paw (Asimina Triloba) can thrive near juglone-producing trees so if you have a black walnut tree consider using it as the key plant in a guild of juglone tolerant plants. One big benefit of this is reduced weed pressure!

- Pruning: Leaves and branches pruned from a tree can be placed on a pile of compost, or left untouched to decompose directly into the soil. Either way, small branches from pruning are the best way to develop healthy fungal activity in the soil. In addition, the tree material such as tree trimmings and scrap wood can be turned into biochar, which is basically charcoal created from biomass by the process of pyrolysis (the decomposition of material due to heat and with an absence of oxygen). The only thing you need to do is to dig a cone-shaped hole and make a fire in it with different sizes of wood. Once the flames die down, and the pile begins to smolder, you just hit it with the hose and completely drench the entire fire down. You can add biochar directly into the garden soil or to the compost pile. Biochar is an important ingredient for a sustainable ecosystem and is one of the best ways to increase soil fertility in the long run.

- Pruning also provides scions for grafting and/or cuttings that could be rooted to propagate more plants

- Trees provide shade. Not only is it ideal for relaxing on hot summer days, but it is also a unique habitat for certain types of crops such as native spinach, nasturtiums, celeriac and chamomile.

- Air: Trees produce oxygen and absorb carbon dioxide from the atmosphere. By switching to a tree-based perennial farming system, we can help fight global warming.

- Windbreak: You can also protect other wind-sensitive crops by trees and bushes as wind blocks.

- Beauty: People often overlook aesthetics in their landscape, but trees add beauty to any area, making it more vibrant and pleasing to the eye.

- Habitat: The more trees we have in our landscape, the more wildlife we have. Bird droppings provide one of the best sources of phosphate, and if you grow trees on your land, you can benefit from this cost-free natural fertilizer that requires zero work.

Edible forests significantly improve production by producing different crops in different layers. Although these systems take time to establish, they offer some of the best opportunities for productive systems to improve soil and ecosystem health. Generally, a food forest contains different "layers" which include the following:

- The canopy layer is composed of large fruit trees and/or nut trees.

- The understory layer consists of smaller nut and fruit trees.

- The shrubs include large perennials, shade-tolerant berries, and mushrooms.

- The herbaceous ground cover layer involves plants such as alpine strawberry, garden sorrel, or other shade-tolerant species,

- The rhizosphere of root crops is full of microorganisms.

- Vines, such as climbing beans and fruits, may form another layer.

- The fungi layer includes edible mushroom species.

Layers of the Edible Forest Garden

1. Canopy/Tall Tree
2. Sub-Canopy/Large Shrub
3. Shrub
4. Herbaceous

5. Ground Cover/Creeper
6. Underground
7. Vertical/Climber

Figure 5.2: Different layers of a forest garden.

Even if you only have a quarter acre of land, you can develop your own food forest to maximize production. Before going out and planting different trees and bushes, ask yourself the following questions:

1. What types of trees grow well in your climate?

2. Which large trees would offer you a large annual harvest while still allowing enough light for other plant species to grow?

3. What types of fruit and nut trees could you plant in the sub-canopy layer?

4. What species could make up the shrub layer, a ground cover layer, root layer, and fungus/mushroom layer?

5. What are some potential opportunities for mutual benefit between the different species you plan to plant?

6. What work will you need to do during the establishment period?

7. How long will it take for you to establish the food forest and when will you get your first harvest?

Taking some time to think about the above questions will help you develop clear and defined goals for building a food forest. It will help you know which direction you want to go in and what you can expect to gain as a result of your efforts.

A Garden Without Neat Rows

It's hard to imagine a garden without rows that is diverse and productive. It is even more difficult to imagine growing a wide array of different crops without spending most of your days kneeling on the ground tilling the soil and weeding out competing plants. It may sound hard to believe, but it's entirely possible to grow a number of plants without rows and the back-breaking labor.

Choosing not to plant our crops in rows might make us lose a sense of order and control, but a disorderly garden is certainly more productive than traditional ones. Planting a diverse set of plants together is always more beneficial, since these plants attract a number of different insects to keep harmful bug populations in check while other non-edible plant species enrich the soil, aiding the growth of robust edible plants.

CUTTING BACK ON THE WORK: THE NO-TILL GARDEN

The most fascinating aspect of a wild garden is that it requires no tilling, pulling weeds, or tampering with the soil. Most farmers consider tilling and weeding to be the two most essential aspects of growing plants, but these methods lead to rapid soil degradation.

The reason wild gardens thrive with minimum human intervention is that these systems function on the same principles as nature itself. The vast number of microorganisms and earthworms present within the soil is more than enough to keep the soil fertile. Similarly, many of the plants that we identify as weeds are essential for maintaining soil fertility and healthy biological activity in the soil. That being said, we don't want an overpopulation of weeds in our garden. Instead of pulling out the weeds from the roots, permaculturists use methods such as mowing and mulching to avoid the overgrowth of weeds. Believe it or not, some weeds are actually beneficial! I prepared a separate eBook for you, that you can download for free:

The Ultimate Guide to Organic Weed Management & How Weeds Can Help Your Yard eBook not only introduces the best and proven organic weed management methods, but also helps to decide which weeds are good, and which weeds are bad for your garden! (Just scan this QR code with your mobile, or visit the link below!)

https://sophiemckay.com/free-resources/

Permaculture relies on systems that are self-sufficient, therefore requiring minimal work on our part. You can build a no-till garden by following the steps given below:

1. Start by loosening the soil with a pitchfork or a hoe. There's no need to turn the soil over: simply loosening the soil will be enough to allow the roots of newly planted crops to penetrate the earth.

2. Layer the ground where you plan to grow crops with cardboard.

3. Create raised beds with bricks, firewood, rocks, or any other large objects.

4. Spread topsoil, mulch, compost, and other organic materials on top of the layer of cardboard.

5. Instead of growing a single crop, plant different crops that complement each other. This is known as "companion planting" and allows greater plant diversity and higher yields. For instance, you can plant tomatoes with basil and marigolds; both these plants repel common pests that attack tomatoes. You can also plant crawling thyme or different kinds of mint plants to help control weed problems. You can protect your tomato plants from deadly pests such as tomato hornworms by growing borage nearby, which also produces

edible flowers and stalks. We will discuss companion planting in more detail in the next chapter.

6. Chop weedy plants, leaving them to decompose on the mulch. Using heavy straw or leaf mulch can also increase soil fertility and prevent weeds from taking over your garden.

PERENNIAL VEGETABLE OPTIONS

Everyone loves tomatoes, cucumbers, zucchinis, and other staple gardens produce, but perennial crops hold numerous advantages over their annual counterparts. The most obvious benefit of perennial crops is that you can enjoy multiple harvests after planting them just once.

Perennial crops work well with no-till gardens as their roots stay in the soil and take away the need to move the soil year after year in order to plant other crops. Furthermore, perennial crops tend to be more nutritious than annuals, easier to grow, and less dependent on frequent irrigation and fertilizers. As their root system develops more thoroughly than annuals, perennials can provide their own nutrition needs and reach deeper sources of groundwater, utilising the water that you slowed, spread, and sank into the ground with your water management.

Perennial plants are also great for ecological sustainability. Their annual leaf fall helps to build soil fertility and contributes to overall soil health. As they develop, perennials are usually adept at resisting pests and other diseases that affect annuals.

Below is a list of ten perennial vegetables that you might consider planting in your no-till garden:

- Rhubarb: This delicious stalk is great for colder climates and is an excellent ingredient for salads and pies.

- Asparagus: This is one of the most common perennial vegetables. While it takes several years to produce edible stalks, once it starts producing it will offer you a plentiful supply of nutritious and delicious vegetables.

- Kale: This superfood is quite the rage among today's health food enthusiasts. Kale will easily reseed itself without any work on your end. Kale is a bi-annual so it would be beneficial to plant them two years in a row so one is always in production while the other goes to seed. There are some perennial kale varieties as well, such as Daubentons.

- Taro root: If you live in warmer climates, this root vegetable provides a nutritious potato substitute that is easy to propagate.

- Jerusalem artichoke: Another perennial tuber, this relative of the sunflower will give you beautiful yellow flowers and tubers that can be eaten raw or cooked like a potato.

- Good King Henry: While some people might consider this to be a common yard weed, the nutritious leaves of this plant make a great perennial substitute for spinach.

- Egyptian onions: These onions, also known as walking onions, produce small bulbs on top of their stalks, which you can eat or replant.

- Ramps: Another traditional annual onion substitute, these wild onions can be harvested from the woods and planted in your raised beds for a steady supply of onions year after year.

- Chipilin: This nitrogen-fixing leaf crop is one of the most nutritious greens you can find for soups and salads. However, it will only grow in zones 8 and up.

- Sorrel: If you like citrus flavors, this lemon-flavored leaf crop will spice up your soups and stews.

Hügelkultur

Another great way to build an elevated garden bed system that maintains long-term soil fertility, is to use a hügelkultur system. The term hügelkultur means "hill culture" and was coined by Austrian organic farmer Sepp Holzer. A hügelkultur bed is a stack of stumps and twigs buried beneath the ground and covered with a layer of hay, straw, or other organic matter. Instead of burning excess wood to clear your land, hügelkultur beds turn excess wood into fertile growing areas.

Hardwood is the best option to achieve this. It adds beneficial organisms such as healthy bacteria and fungi to speed up the decomposition process. Conifers such as cedar and pine are extremely difficult to break down and lead to "brown rot," a type of fungus that can impair plant growth. Like all organic matter, wood slowly decomposes in the soil. Billions of bacteria, mycelium, and other creatures slowly colonize all types of wood then return to topsoil. Therefore, hügelkultur beds help soil organisms break down organic matter by providing them a concentrated amount of food material.

Placing large amounts of stumps, branches, and other wood-based materials in one spot will invite several different organisms to that particular area. Mulch and litter become fertile soil layers within a few months, but it takes years for soil organisms to turn a pile of trees into soil. You can plant crops on beds or piles of slowly decomposed trees. Tree trunks and branches in hügelkultur beds act as a constant source of nutrition, fertilizing the plant for several years.

Covering the hügelkultur bed with topsoil, finished compost, and mulch creates a medium in which almost any crop can be planted. These beds also retain large amounts of water. If you have come across rotting wood logs in the forest, you know how they feel damp to the touch even in a severe drought. Hügelkultur beds, therefore, hold water in the same way and create a small reservoir that can be used by plants even during long dry spells.

The hügelkultur system recycles unwanted timber, turning it into an important part of our little agricultural system. The figure below illustrates a typical hügelkultur system.

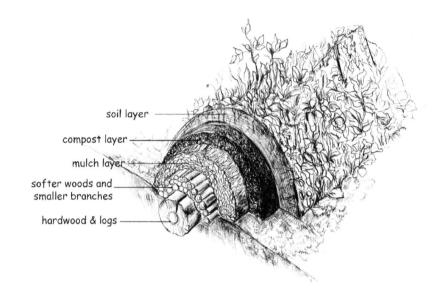

soil layer

compost layer

mulch layer

softer woods and smaller branches

hardwood & logs

Figure 5.3: Hügelkultur bed.

In addition, the beds allow you to integrate a wide variety of design elements into your landscape. For example, suppose you only have a small backyard adjacent to a row of trees. You can easily collect enough wood from the fallen limbs to make a series of raised garden beds. Instead of spreading compost on the bed every year, the wood that slowly rots inside the hügelkultur mounds keeps the soil fertile for many years. If you live and cultivate on slopes, you can also integrate these mounds into your landscape by placing the hügelkultur beds on the contours of the slopes. You can dig swales and drains on the contour and use the excavated soil to cover the branches.

Regardless of the design of the hügelkultur bed, the basic process is the same. Look for large numbers of hardwood branches and stumps. Place the wood where you want to make a garden bed and cover it with upside-down grass, soil, compost, and mulch. General tip: remember to keep your nitrogen levels up at first. If you use decaying wood it won't be an issue but if the wood is pretty fresh it may suck a lot of the nitrogen up in order to decompose the high carbon content in the logs.

Raised Beds

Raised beds are my personal favorite permaculture method, because they can easily transform a small space into a lush vegetable garden. They're great for people with back problems or knee injuries and the elderly, since these garden beds are above ground level as well as involve minimal labor.

Raised beds can be described as planting beds that elevate the soil level. They can be made from different materials and vary in height, ranging anywhere from a couple of inches to waist high. Since the planting beds are raised above the ground, there's plenty of room around them for you to walk. This prevents the soil from becoming compact, keeping it fluffy and loose instead. The raised edges also make it more difficult for creeping weeds to find their way into your beautiful garden soil.

Usually, raised beds have frames that are either made from wood, metal or hard plastic. Based on your personal preference, however, you can also choose cinder blocks, stone, or cement as the material for making the frames. You can also control soil temperature by choosing the right color of raised beds. In colder climates we use darker materials for beds where we grow vegetables like peppers that prefer warmer soils. Using a lighter color would limit the heat gains. Regardless of the material from which it's made, the perfect raised bed is narrow enough for you to reach the center from both with an average width of four feet or less. They can have different depths depending on the kinds of plants that you plan to grow. For example, miniature fruit trees and tomatoes have extensive root systems that require deep beds with more soil, while lettuce and pansies are shallow-rooted plants that don't require as much soil.

Generally, raised beds don't have a bottom, although it can be beneficial to have one made from fine mesh hardware cloth to keep out gophers and other burrowing rodents. They can be made with a solid bottom, which is perfect for keeping them on a patio or deck; however, it's important to ensure proper drainage. Holes can be drilled into the solid bottom to allow the drainage of excess water.

The Royal Horticultural Society recommends lining three inches of stones or coarse gravel covered with a geotextile membrane (a permeable fabric) underneath raised beds built over concrete. Due to the presence of the membrane, the stones and gravel do not get mixed with soil, which also prevents clogging.

A raised garden bed provides you with the perfect opportunity to manipulate the microclimate for your plants. By building raised beds, you can control soil nutrients, improve drainage and prevent soil erosion.

Moreover, by using raised beds, you can maximize available space, so raised beds are a fantastic opportunity for growers that have a small backyard to make the most with small spaces. You can grow a dense plantation with the plants growing close to each other, which prevents weeds. Another benefit of using raised beds is that they warm up quickly during spring, extending the growing season. They also provide good drainage, which prevents the soil from becoming waterlogged during heavy rainfall, protecting the plant roots.

While there are numerous advantages of raised bed gardens, it's important to consider a few challenges that these structures may present. Because raised beds are quick to absorb and retain heat, the soil may dry out quicker during the summer months, which means they require frequent irrigation. Furthermore, a dense plantation may increase crop yield but may give rise to foliar diseases due to miss out on some vegetable varieties. Lastly, the cost ~~~~~~~~ up raised beds is a lot more than traditional farming. However, there are ways to bring down the cost by using recycled materials such as decking, old tyres, and logs stacked on stumps.

Despite all these challenges, the benefits of a raised bed garden outweigh the disadvantages in many cases. Not to mention, you can work your way around most problems. For example, you can use drip irrigation instead of overhead watering to prevent the soil from drying out and avoid foliar diseases. Similarly, you can choose vines that are more compact or use a trellis. Moreover, you can bring down the cost by choosing inexpensive materials for the frame such as concrete or searching local marketplaces for unwanted rocks/bricks/interlocking bricks from an old driveway/walkway. The next figure illustrates a typical raised garden bed.

Figure 5.4: Raised bed with some hügelkultur properties.

BUILDING RAISED BEDS

When it comes to building raised beds, I always start by finding the right location. Ideally, a raised bed should be constructed in a spot that receives at least six to eight hours of sunlight. Analyze the soil where you plan to build the garden bed; it's best to avoid marshy areas that can result in poor drainage unless you are growing plants that like "wet feet". Let's look at the different steps involved in constructing raised beds.

Step 1: Figure Out the Dimensions of the Frame

While there is no limit on the length of the frame, you should aim for no more than forty-eight inches in width and make sure that you can reach the middle from either side. As I mentioned previously, the height of the frame depends entirely on the kind of plants you want to grow, your ability to bend over, and how much material you can find to fill your bed.

Step 2: Get Digging!

If the ground where you plan to build the raised bed has never been used for gardening before, start digging it to a depth of at least sixteen inches. Watch out for any roots underneath the soil and remove them. Make a pile of them in the center so you won't run into any obstructions when you're setting up the bed. If you don't want the extra work, then you can skip the shovel and mow the area instead. If you're working in a lawn, you can skip the digging and mowing altogether.

Step 3: Start Building the Frames

There are a lot of options to choose from when it comes to choosing the right material for the framing. The decision mostly comes down to how much you're willing to spend. Concrete blocks and pressure-treated lumber such as cedar falls on the cheaper side, while pricier options include stones or bricks.

If you decide to go for lumber, then it's best to construct the frame with posts that can help keep the structure stable or build a trench at least a few inches deep to maintain balance. Remember that you should be able to reach all the plants so you can harvest or water with ease. For this reason, the bed layout should not be wider than three or four feet. Furthermore, your garden bed should ideally be almost a foot deep. As a minimum, however, for deep-rooted plants, it should have a depth of eighteen inches minimum. If you plan to use treated wood for building your garden bed, then remember to line the lumber to avoid toxic chemicals from the treated wood seeping into the soil and polluting the ground.

Step 4: Add the Soil

Spread an even layer of soil, add soil amendments (if you'd planned to), and pour water to make everything settle in place. Rake the bed to make sure the soil's even before planting and go for an ideal soil mix that contains half garden soil and half compost.

Step 5: Build Pathways

Pathways that are twenty-four inches wide will allow you to walk between the garden bed and tend to your plants with ease. If you are growing grass between your beds consider the width of your lawn mower if you are going to use it in this space. Another great idea is to cover the pathways with a weed barrier that has a two- to three-inch layer of bark, gravel, or sawdust on top. Alternatively, you can cover it with turf.

Step 6: Keep Your Feet Off the Bed!

Lay down some ground rules about not stepping on the bed to reduce compaction, since walking on the soil inside the raised bed defeats the purpose of this gardening structure. It can reduce aeration and have an adverse effect on root growth.

Choosing the Best Plants for Your Permaculture Garden

By using permaculture techniques, you can create a lush, healthy garden, cut down your carbon footprint and boost local insect populations, but your success largely depends on choosing the right plants. The weather conditions at the place where you live are obviously an important deciding factor about what plants you can grow in your permaculture garden.

In this book, we're going to look at plants that grow best in temperate climates of North America and Europe. Please make sure to look up plant varieties suited to the climate of the area that you live in to find the perfect plants for your permaculture garden. However, there are some plants that bear the universal characteristics of great plants for permaculture that you can grow regardless of the climate. Let's look at some of these characteristics.

Low Maintenance

The best thing about permaculture gardens is that they don't require a lot of work. So it's safe to assume that hardy, low-maintenance plants are a defining feature of a permaculture garden. Plants that can adjust themselves to less than ideal conditions such as nutrient poor soil or extreme weather are great candidates for your permaculture garden.

Deep Rooted Plants

If you don't have a nutrient-rich topsoil then don't despair. You can go deep-rooted plants, since they can reach deep into the soil and extract nutrients.

Plants in the Legume Family

Legumes are a top favorite for growing in permaculture gardens because of their nitrogen-fixing ability.

Plants with Dense Foliage

Plants with lush, green, dense leaves are an excellent option for permaculture gardens, since they're great for making mulch. Some of these plants can be classified as "living mulch," because they help lock in moisture in the soil and prevent the growth of weeds by blocking sunlight. Others can be pruned and their branches can then serve as mulch.

Now that we know what factors make a plant perfect for a permaculture garden, let's look at some plants that are well-suited for permaculture.

1. **Comfrey**

   Many farmers consider this non-edible plant a weed, but the characteristics that make it a tough and fast-growing plant are exactly what makes it so perfect for your permaculture garden. The deep taproots of this plant can reach up to two meters into the ground and access minerals buried deep in the subsoil, bringing them up to the surface for other plants to benefit. This plant has several medicinal properties, produces large quantities of biomass and attracts bees. Lastly, the leaves of this plant can be used as mulch, compost or animal fodder.

2. **Hazelnut**

   These small trees make excellent windbreaks and can be planted with larger trees such as apples to build permaculture guilds, which is the process of growing trees and plants in groups. These shade tolerant plants last up to fifty years and produce high-calorie nuts that can be consumed raw, roasted or ground to produce flour or extract oil. Hazelnuts will live for up to fifty years and make a great addition to your food forest.

3. **Jerusalem Artichoke**

   The hardy nature of these plants makes them a great pick for permaculture gardens. They are low maintenance and don't require a lot of water. They resemble sunflowers and produce sturdy, tall stems that can act like a trellis for climbing plants.

4. **Fiddleheads**

   These ferns taste the same as asparagus after being cooked. However, they're edible only in spring before their fronds begin to unfurl. Eating other varieties could be dangerous, so make sure to identify them correctly! They're packed with nutrients and vitamins, providing you with the necessary nourishment while you wait for your other plants to mature.

5. **Mulberry**

You can eat these delicious berries simply by plucking them from the trees or using them to make jams. Mulberry trees are quick to grow and mature into extremely strong trees that draw many species of birds and wild animals while their large, broad leaves make them perfect for making mulch.

6. **Mint**

This famous plant is a popular culinary ingredient that has multiple benefits. It is nutrient rich, great for getting rid of bad breath and provides an excellent remedy for indigestion. It grows like a weed and serves as living mulch when grown underneath tall plants. Another advantage of planting mint in your permaculture garden is that it draws in the honey bees while keeping harmful bugs out. It's also common for gardeners to grow it in pots (sometimes sunk into the ground) because of its tendency to spread very rapidly.

7. **Arrowhead**

This water vegetable is a delicious tuber that is eaten after boiling or roasting (never raw). It requires a bit of work to grow, but is worth the effort. It's a great option if you have a pond on your land. Growing near a water body, this nutty flavored vegetable creates a shady spot for frogs, turtles and other bug-eating animals to gather around.

8. **Asparagus**

This slow-growing plant takes up to three years to mature, but once you plant this in your garden, it will keep coming back bigger and better every year. However, you may notice a drop in yield after fifteen years. It's low-maintenance once it adjusts to the garden, and also keeps away parasites such as nematodes, making it a perfect companion plant to grow alongside tomatoes.

Apart from the crops mentioned above, other plants that are excellent for permaculture gardens include red clover, wild leeks, strawberries, stinging nettle, walking onions, black locust and hops. Edible flowers such as chrysanthemums, hibiscus, violets, magnolia and nasturtiums can also serve as great permaculture plants.

What Makes Nitrogen-Fixing Plants Important?

Have you ever wondered how nature continues to provide us with an abundance of food in the wild, without depending on any outside sources of nutrition, how it goes on working like clockwork without any meddling on our behalf?

Nature provides for itself. It replenishes lost nutrients by accumulating organic matter which protects the soil, builds humus, and increases the activity of soil organisms. The abundance of nitrogen in the air fulfills another important plant nutrient requirement.

Almost 70% of the air is made up of nitrogen, and almost every plant requires a steady supply of nitrogen to flourish. So how could nature trap the nitrogen from the air into the soil for the plants?

The leaves of nitrogen-fixing plants absorb the nitrogen floating in the air and "fix" it in the soil. The process takes place in the nodules present on the roots of these hard-working plants, making them crucial for the survival of many crops. Beans and peas are some examples of nitrogen-fixing plants. If you've ever had a look at the roots of a bean plant, then you may have seen several tiny white nodules on the roots. Those nodules contain pure nitrogen, which improves soil health. Even after the bean plant's death, the nitrogen produced in the nodules remains in the soil, enriching its surroundings.

In addition to leguminous plants such as beans and peas, there are nitrogen-fixing trees and shrubs as well. Pruning of these trees and bushes makes them shed their root systems, adding nitrogen to the soil. This is why, in the past, many agrarian societies such as the Mayans designed planting systems which paired a carbohydrate crop with heavy nutrient requirements such as corn or wheat with leguminous crops that could add nitrogen to the soil.

Some popular combinations of plants that you can use include squash, beans and corn, also known as "the three sisters". You can also plant alfalfa, vetch, or winter peas. Alfalfa is a nitrogen-fixing cover crop, while winter peas can be plowed into the ground, increasing soil fertility and organic matter content.

Agriculture systems based on perennial trees include nitrogen-fixing trees and shrubs that you can plant together with nut and fruit trees in your orchard. These trees are essential for keeping the soil fertile and for providing the nutrients for the growth of other trees. Moreover, they can withstand heavy pruning, so plant growers can rest assured that these highly beneficial trees will not outcompete other plants and cast a heavy shade.

BEST NITROGEN-FIXING TREES AND BUSHES FOR PERMACULTURE GARDENS

Apart from improving nutrient content in the soil, nitrogen-fixing trees and bushes are important sources of food and fuel, making them an essential component of the permaculture garden. Here is a list of some nitrogen-fixing trees and shrubs and their characteristics:

- Goumi: This nitrogen-fixing bush produces tasty red berries that are great for jams or jellies.

- Seaberry or sea buckthorn: This nitrogen-fixing bush offers extremely nutrient-dense yellow fruits that are high in vitamin C and antioxidants.

- Chipilin: Another nitrogen-fixing bush that provides a protein-dense green leaf that can be eaten in soups or salads.

- Alder: These trees not only fix nitrogen, they also increase organic matter content in the soil as their leaves fall and decompose on the ground. Moreover, they're a source of firewood.

- Black locust: In addition to providing firewood, this rapidly growing tree responds well to heavy pruning and gives fragrant flowers that draw bees, aiding the pollination process.

Building Your Own Nursery

A tree-based agriculture system can be quite expensive to set up initially. Moreover, you may feel tempted to forgo all the hard work and save money by simply buying a $30 bag of fruit at a nearby orchard instead. Before you give up on your dream of sustainable living, here's an idea about how you can shave the cost of building a permaculture garden or a food forest.

An excellent way to bring down the price of setting up your own agriculture system is to buy a few plants and propagate them to get more plants. Planting seeds is the easiest propagation technique. Most nitrogen-fixing trees and bushes can be grown by sowing seeds, but some species prefer vegetative techniques such as grafting, layering and air grafting.

Making your own plant nursery can help you save thousands of dollars. It can help you store desired genetic traits that you can use to diversify the plant species on your land and amplify the best characteristics in your plants. Moreover, you can sell some of the plants that you propagate and earn money. By setting up a nursery, you can use your land to generate profits, which allow you to cover the cost of setting up a permaculture garden and save for the future.

If you don't have a parent plant to start with, you can simply buy a root stock at a fairly low price. Once you have the root stock, all you need is a single established tree that will offer you the scions required for grafting onto the root stock. So a good way to start the nursery is to buy one or two different types of fruit or nut trees or any ornamental plants that you intend to sell. Keeping a variety of tree that will produce seed for rootstock may be helpful down the road. American Plum, Antanovka Apple and Bartlett Pear are all cold hardy varieties that grow true to seed and work well as rootstock so it yields both edible fruit and seeds to grow more trees.

Permaculture in Small Spaces: Making an Urban Garden

Building a food forest might seem like a great idea, but what if you don't have several acres of abandoned land to begin your permaculture design? Though a lack of access to a decent portion of land is certainly a challenge for many people, the permaculture principles, elements of design, and production tools can certainly be used in an urban setting. You can start your urban garden by placing a few raised beds, pots or containers on your balcony or patio.

A prerequisite for the rapid construction of soil is a large amount of organic matter. Living in the countryside provides a lot of litter, twigs, and branches for wood chips, and straw from previous wheat harvests, but it's not easy. You need to go out and scrape the leaves, collect twigs and branches to make mulch, or plant and harvest wheat to make the straw.

But in almost every city, there are enormous amounts of organic matter along the curb of any street. One of the most ironic behaviors of urban dwellers is their hatred for fallen leaves. People pay a lot of money to allow a group of young people with rakes and blowers to put the leaves in plastic trash bags and put them on the sidewalk so that garbage trucks can get rid of them. Similarly, fallen tree branches are cut to a manageable size with a chainsaw and left for the trash truck.

Power companies with industrial-sized woodcutters make stunning piles of wood chips from branches and twigs cut from trees that obstruct power lines running through the city. Driving around town, it's easy to find enough organic matter to turn even hard clay soil into fertile humus.

A general rule of thumb for permaculture, and for gardening in general, is to choose those plants that you love. This will keep you interested and make work feel like a breeze as you tend to your favorite plants in your garden. Now that you know exactly what to grow and how to grow it, it's time to talk about harvesting the crops. Chapter 6 is all about improving yields and bringing food to the table.

CHAPTER 6

From the Garden to Your Table

I magine yourself walking out in your backyard to pick a handful of fresh, ripe strawberries or redcurrants to put in your bowl of oatmeal for breakfast or strolling onto your patio to pluck some lush, green salads for lunch. What would it be like to have all your food growing just a few steps away?

A few years ago, the idea that I could grow my own food felt completely foreign to me. Now that I have a functioning permaculture garden in place, I love how convenient it is for me to find everything that I'd need for making dinner simply a few steps away. Not to mention, it has made a huge impact on my finances, as I'm now saving more than ever.

Initially, I started with a 30 by 25 ft (9 by 8 m) piece of land where I planted a wide range of fruits, vegetables, edible flowers, and herbs. I used some ingenious permaculture techniques to achieve a high yield of diverse plants. Here are some of the strategies that I used to achieve my targets.

1. NOURISH YOUR SOIL

I find it rather amusing sometimes that despite our many accomplishments in science and technology, our survival still depends on a six-inch layer of topsoil. Some of the greatest civilizations came to an untimely demise due to long spells of drought or the destruction of fertile topsoil. Soil holds the key to higher crop yield, making it an essential part of your permaculture system that you should pay the most attention to.

I started my permaculture garden by building two 5 by 5 ft (1,5 by 1,5 m) raised beds with wooden frames. I used scaffolding planks to make them and placed the finished raised beds in a sunny spot in the garden. I spread a layer of wood chips at the bottom of each bed, then added a mix of soil and manure on top. The reason I lined the bottom with wood chips was to increase biomass (and also because it was the only thing that I had available at that time). When I inspected the soil a few months later, I was delighted to see that the wood chips had broken down completely and given rise to mycorrhizal fungi, which helped transport nutrients to the plants' roots, leading to higher yields.

Another trick that greatly improved crop yield for me was making sure not to step on the soil in raised beds and allowing worms and microorganisms to do all the work instead of tilling the soil myself. I fertilized the soil regularly by making my own compost from kitchen wastes and chicken manure and used the same compost as mulch during spring and autumn.

Because of these techniques, I was able to keep the topsoil fertile and harvested a generous amount of vegetables throughout the year to feed my family. So don't feel disheartened if you only have a small patch of land to work with. By implementing the right techniques, you can turn the smallest places into a permaculture garden and grow food in surplus.

2. BUILDING THE RIGHT SHAPED RAISED BEDS

The shape of your raised beds can have a profound impact on plant yield. A dome-shaped bed with sloping sides gives you more surface area to work with than others. For instance, if the width of the bed is five feet (1,5m) at the base, you can get a six-foot-wide (1,8m) arch of soil. This gives you more control over the microclimates in your raised bed and you can manipulate different environmental factors to help different plants flourish in the same space.

As a result, you can grow diverse varieties of plants without worrying that you'll run out of land. Since some plants love shady areas while others prefer bright sunny spots, increasing the surface area of your raised beds by changing the shape of the frame is a great way to grow plants with different requirements.

I mentioned above how I began my journey towards self-sufficiency with just two raised garden beds in my garden. When I had the chance to build a new bed, I decided to go for a more dome-shaped design. I planted chestnuts along the edges to hold onto the soil, grew asparagus on the south-facing edge, strawberries on the north, and grew kale, chard, and beans in the center. I had the biggest success with strawberries and I could easily pick them. I also harvested a good amount of chard, asparagus, beans and beetroot in the summer months and kale during winter.

3. TESSELLATE

Growing crops in neat little rows leave a lot of land unused. So it's no wonder that we don't see any symmetrical rows in nature; in the wild, nothing is wasted. Nature leaves no empty spaces between the plants by growing them in a tessellating pattern, almost as if Mother Nature is busy playing a game of Tetris.

Since permaculture teaches us to imitate nature as best as possible to gain maximum benefit, growing plants in triangle formations is a unique feature of a permaculture garden that results in higher yields.

For example, if you're thinking about planting broad beans, the instructions on the packet say that you should leave about nine inches of space between the plants. What I like to do is that I use a dibber to make the outline of a triangle with at least nine inches of space between each corner. On each corner, I dig a hole and plant the beans.

This means I get to plant almost 10% more plants in the same space, which may not seem like much, but it can have a huge impact on crop yield.

4. GROW VERTICALLY

Stacking crops is a permaculture technique that involves growing crops in layers. If you walk into a forest, you'll see plants growing in layers covering every inch of space from the ground to the tree canopy. We can follow this natural pattern by stacking crops instead of mono-cropping. I use this technique in two ways: I train climbing vegetables on a trellis in raised beds and grow shrubs and climbing vines up to fruit trees in the rest of the garden.

Vegetables such as beans, cucumbers, and peas can be easily trained over a trellis or poles, giving you more room to grow other vegetables such as salads, beetroot, or chard. In the rest of the garden, you can plant a layer of strawberries on the ground, grow a shrub layer of currants and raspberries, while climbing vines such as bayberries, wineberries, and loganberries can be trained up on the fences. Fruits such as apples and pears occupy the canopy layer and some plants such as lemongrass, mint, and coriander can be grown in hanging baskets.

5. GROW COMPANION PLANTS

Companion planting involves growing a set of compatible plants close to one another, so each plant can benefit from the properties of the other. These benefits include pollination, pest control, maximizing use of space, providing habitat for beneficial insects, and increasing crop productivity.

Plant	Good companions	Bad companions
Asparagus	Basil, Marigold, Parsley, Dill, Tomato, Nasturtium	Garlic, Potato, Onions
Beans	Potato, Marigold, Cucumbers, Squash, Summer Savory, Corn	Tomato, Pepper, Chives, Garlic, Onions
Beets	Mint, Garlic, Onions, Leeks, Scallon, Broccoli, Cauliflower, Brussels sprouts, Radish, Kale, Cabbage	Pole beans
Broccoli	Dill, Mint, Rosemary	Strawberry, Mustard, Tomato, Oregano
Cabbage	Onions, Dill, Oregano, Sage, Mint, Chamomille, Nasturtium, Clover, Beets	Strawberry, Tomato, Peppers, Eggplant
Corn	Cucumber, Beans, Melons, Parsley, Squash, Marigold, Pumpkin	Tomato
Cucumber	Radish, Lettuce, Onions, Dill, Nasturtium, Corn, Beans	Potato, Sage
Eggplant	Catnip, Spinach, Peppers, Nasturtium, Marigold, Sunflower, Bush beans, Thyme, Tarragon, Tomato, Potato	Fennel
Lettuce	Radish, Dill, Cucumber, Carrot, Strawberry	Beans, Beets, Cabbage, Parsley
Peppers	Beans, Tomato, Onions, Geranium, Petunia	Fennel
Potato	Eggplant, Beans, Cabbage, Peas, Sage, Corn, Nasturtium, Catnip, Coriander	Cucumber, Tomato, Pumpkin, Spinach, Fennel, Onions, Squash, Fennel, Raspberries
Pumpkin	Melons, Corn, Dill, Radish, Beans, Oregano	Potato
Spinach	Cauliflower, Strawberry, Radish, Eggplant	Potato
Squash	Onion, Corn, Mint, Nasturtium, Dill, Peas, Beans, Radish	Potato
Tomato	Carrot, Parsley, Basil, Marigold, Garlic,Asparagus, Collards	Corn, Cabbage, Broccoli, Brussels sprouts, Potato
Turnip	Radish, Cauliflower, Beans, Lettuce, Spinach, Broccoli, Cabbage, Peas, Tomato, Brussels sprouts, Mint	Carrot, Parsley and other root crops
Zucchini	Nasturtium, Corn, Beans	Potato

Figure 6.1: Companion plants.

In my garden, I have planted the classic Native American combination called "the three sisters": climbing beans, squash, and sweetcorn. The sturdy sweetcorn stalks are great for climbing beans while the nitrogen-fixing characteristic of the beans improves nutrient content in the soil, which benefits sweetcorn. Squash grows in between the sweetcorn and beans, keeping moisture in the soil to prevent the growth of weeds.

Another plant that I like to grow along with the three sisters is a nasturtium. Some other combinations include:

- Growing climbing beans with nasturtium carpeting the ground to draw black fly, keeping them away from the beans.

- Planting radish and parsnip together. Radish can be harvested quickly while parsnip takes some time to mature.

- Onions and carrots since the smell of onions keep the carrot flies away.

- Planting various herbs and vegetables together to keep away the pests that could harm the vegetables such as cabbage white butterflies.

6. GO FOR PLANT GUILDS

A group of plants that benefit each other is called a guild. They consist of a whole set of plants that work as a group, typically centered around a key plant (often a tree). Not only can you save space by planting these plants together, but you can also significantly increase your yield.

Guilds tend to mimic forest patterns. In a forest, there is usually an anchor species such as a tree or a plant which lies at the center of a natural-occurring guild. Various plant and fungi species surround the anchor and receive support from it like keeping pests away, bringing in pollinators and providing shade. The plants growing around the anchor also provide a number of benefits to each other and the tree or plant growing in the center.

For example, an apple tree can act as the anchor and its trunk can be used to grow climbing plants like peas, which will also add nitrogen to the soil, while carrots can be grown around the tree to keep the soil loose so the tree's roots can extend downward. Some other plants that can be grown around the apple tree are clovers (weed suppressant, ground cover and nitrogen-fixer), raspberry shrubs (wind protection), marigolds and daisies (attract pollinators), and onions (deter pests). Another benefit in the North: Planting a shrub to the south of a fruit tree can prevent trees from getting sun burnt in the winter. This happens when the low sun bounces off of the snow and can cook the trunks of your trees.

7. GROWING CROPS IN SUCCESSION

Growing plants in a successive order gives the opportunity to grow multiple crops in the same space, maximizing yield in the growing season. Even living in the fairly cold climate of Europe, I was able to grow three different crops in the same area over a year. I would begin by planting an early crop of purple podded peas and follow that with a quick crop of summer salads, then I'd plant broad beans in the autumn, which I could harvest in winter.

Plant varieties that are quick to mature provide you with enough food during each season. Sowing different plants in succession gives us something to harvest throughout the year while replenishing the soil with fresh compost and mulch helps maintain soil fertility. You can plant cut-and-come-again salads and cut the young leaves to delay the plant's maturation. This way you can enjoy multiple harvests of small, mild-flavored leaves for a long time. Some examples of cut-and-come-again plants include purple sprouting broccoli, red kale, rocket, sorrel, and spinach.

8. EXTENDING THE GROWING SEASON

I've placed my raised beds in a sunny spot so that it soaks up the heat from the sun, making it warm up quickly during spring and remain warm for a long time in autumn. Some other ways to stretch the growing season include placing a cloche (bell shade) over the plants for protection from harsh weather spells, growing seedlings in a cold frame, and transferring them to the soil outside as soon as warm weather arrives.

Covering the soil with black plastic just before spring also helps the soil absorb heat quickly. If you have a large, empty space available then you can set up a polytunnel or greenhouse, which are both great for extending the growing season.

Knowing your plants is essential if you want to maximize yield by adjusting different environmental factors. Once I learned that the Ragged Jack or Red Russian variety of kale can be grown through overwintering, I went ahead and planted it in December. As soon as the days got longer in the new year, I was rewarded with fresh green leaves and delicious flowering shoots.

Another plant that quickly became the highlight of my garden during winters was perennial broccoli. The white florets would appear quite quickly in early spring.

It's safe to say that perennials prove extremely useful in a permaculture garden with their quick harvests and high yields. For example, rhubarbs and red currants would keep your kitchen table full while you wait for your annual crops to mature. Sorrel is another favorite of mine, which I use frequently in salads. Ramsons (commonly known as ramps or wild garlic) are also a great plant to grow under fruit trees.

9. INCREASE THE VALUE OF YOUR PLANTS

You can make your harvests more valuable by going for plants that are expensive in the shops. Organic asparagus, blueberries, potatoes, tomatoes and strawberries are some examples of costly crops that you can easily grow in your backyard.

I get immense satisfaction from being able to bring in super-fresh produce from my garden, making me value the plants I grow all the more. Many fruits and vegetables take only a few hours to deteriorate despite the plastic packaging. Salad leaves and raspberries are examples of this.

A prickly cucumber that's still warm to the touch or a vegetable variety that hasn't even made its way to the supermarket yet are some other examples that make it hard to put a price tag on permaculture.

10. LOVE WHAT YOU DO

At the end of the day, permaculture is all about using your imagination to envision a self-sustaining garden that requires the least amount of work. And you can only achieve this if you let go of past beliefs and let your creative spirit fly.

The sense of fulfillment and joy that comes from watching your plants grow is incomparable. Doing what you love boosts your mental wellbeing. Research has shown that gardening leads to numerous benefits such as reducing stress, improving mood, and reducing symptoms of depression and anxiety. For example, I love that I get a bit of gentle exercise as I tend to the plants in my garden while listening to birdsong. While I can't exchange this experience for material wealth, it is certainly good for my mind, body, and soul and contributes toward community building, which are all things that I consider as important as yields or financial gains.

Storing Excess Food

So far, we've been focusing on techniques for increasing yields and getting more harvest. But what happens when you end up with more food than you need? Luckily, there are a number of different ways that you can store surplus food and use it later. Let's look at some food storage ideas.

CANNING

My personal favorite technique to store food is canning. I find it so fun, rewarding and practical that I enjoy every second of it. I use fresh produce from my garden to make large pots of delicious and healthy sauces such as spaghetti sauce and enchilada sauce and then I preserve them with canning. This way I can put surplus tomatoes to good use and quickly make dinner. I also store homemade jams, jellies, artichoke hearts and roasted hatch chillis in cans, so I can stack them in the pantry instead of having them take up space in the freezer.

The canning process has several stages: cleaning and preparing the food; blanching; filling the containers; and sealing the containers. Blanching fruits and vegetables, by immersing them in hot water or using steam, softens them and deactivates enzymes that could cause the canned food to spoil. The National Center for Home Food Preservation recommends sterilizing jars by immersing them in boiling water for 10 minutes. The jars should also be sterilized before filling them with produce by filling clean, empty jars with water and boiling for 10 minutes. It's also important to store the jars below 95°F (35C°). The best quality retention can be obtained by storying jars between 50° and 70°F (12-24 C°).

Moreover, all low-acid foods such as red meats, milk, sea foods and all vegetables except tomatoes must be sterilized at temperatures of 240° to 250°F (115– 120 C°), which can be achieved with pressure canners. The canner has to be operated at 10 to 15 PSIG (pounds per square inch of pressure as measured by gauge) for 20 to 100 minutes to destroy harmful bacteria (National Center for Home Food Preservation, 2017.).

Through canning, you can preserve a number of different fruits and vegetables and enjoy them as spreads or sauces throughout the year.

FREEZING

The most obvious way to preserve food over a long time is simply by stashing it away in the freezer. You can store a wide variety of fruits and vegetables this way. You may have to wash, clean and chop some of the food to keep it fresh, but the effort is definitely worth it. I like to shell peas and freeze them in airtight bags. The same goes for broccoli, cauliflower and eggplant.

I find that vegetables tend to get mushy after defrosting, so blanching them before putting them in the freezer is a good idea to help prevent this. In the case of eggplant, I either pan fry it or cut it in cubes and steam before freezing to keep it fresh. I later take it out and let it thaw then use it to make eggplant enchilada or eggplant parmesan.

With cauliflower and broccoli, I simply steam the florets before freezing. The frozen vegetables are great for making quiche later on. Some other foods that do well in the freezer are: chevre (goat cheese), salsa, pesto, and berries.

DEHYDRATING

Another excellent food preservation technique is dehydration, so investing in a dehydrator is a great idea. All you need to do is to pop the food in the dehydrator, let it cool, then toss it in an airtight bag. DIY solar dehydrators are a great option and you can add one 100 watt light bulb in it to add heat during the colder fall days. Also, Freeze dryers are expensive but preserve much more of the nutritional content while having a shelf life of 25 years. Dried fruits can be stored this way so you can snack on them all year long. Moreover, you can even dry out orange peels to make your very own source of vitamin C in the form of citrus powder. Some other foods that can be stored by dehydration include bananas, apples, cranberries, cherries, kiwis, oranges, plums and tomatoes.

By now you have a good idea about how to set up a permaculture garden, successfully grow your own food, work your way around roadblocks, maximize yields and store the excess. Let's now look at community building and how permaculture contributes to strengthening the local economy. Chapter 7 is all about sharing with your community and helping others.

CHAPTER 7

Continued Success and Financial Profits

I want you to take a moment and imagine yourself in the shoes of a single parent who works a minimum-wage job. She lives in a small town in Vermont in a tiny, rented apartment and her weekly food budget uses up almost half of her income. Paying off her car loan and the money she spends on gas takes another big chunk from her salary, so by the end of the month, she's left with no money. If you look at where the cash that she spends goes, you'd realize that a very small amount of what she earns goes to the community where she lives.

Companies that benefit from her paycheck include real estate companies in the capital, banks with headquarters in the big cities, and the oil giants in countries on the other side of the world. The money she works so hard to earn quickly flows out of the small town that she's in, doing nothing to improve the living conditions of her community and instead making its way back into the pockets of financial giants.

Helping your community and sharing your profit with others strengthens your business ventures. Establishing strong community ties is crucial for your emotional and mental wellbeing. If you find yourself ending up with surplus food, then try sharing some with your neighbors or selling it at a reduced rate. You won't have to worry about storage and you'd create feelings of goodwill within the community. You can even barter food items for different services.

Maximize Your Profits

Once you've perfected your permaculture design and established a fully functional agricultural system, it's time to start focusing on bringing in profits. While permaculture principles center around being selfless and sharing our success with others, profitability is essential to keep a business venture going for a long time. Here are some tips to help you bring in the profits:

1. **Grow Profitable Plants**
   Ginseng, garlic, rhubarb and mushrooms are some examples of plants that come with a high price tag. Herbs such as oregano, basil, chives, cilantro, and lavender are always popular, so it's a good idea to grow them on your land.

2. **Grow Seasonal Decorative Plants**
   Seasonal plants with bright, colorful flowers are quick to sell out. Marigolds, chrysanthemums, hostas, orange daylilies, and ornamental kale are some gorgeous seasonal varieties that help boost sales.

3. **Sell Preserved Fruits and Vegetables**
   Selling the food that you've preserved out of season is a sure way to attract a lot of customers. Fruit jams, canned tomato paste, and beans are some items that are bound to sell out in a matter of minutes.

4. **Grow Beautiful Flowers**

   Gorgeous flower bouquets are a must on every occasion and you can easily tap into this revenue stream by growing beautiful, bright-colored flowers like roses, geraniums, or daisies.

5. **Eggs**

   Keeping a few chickens on your land can come in handy in many ways. Eggs are a breakfast staple while chicken manure can be used to make fertilizer.

6. **Nursery of Local Trees**

   Selling bagged fruits or juice from your fruit orchard is also an excellent way to generate revenue.

Taking charge of your own food supply and generating enough profits from it to become financially stable can feel incredibly empowering. Following the principles of permaculture and the tips in this book can help you establish a profitable business and follow your passion as a nature lover. Let's have a quick recap of the different factors that can help you maintain long-term success:

1. Keep optimizing your design and correcting any minor malfunctions as you go along. Keep learning and perfecting your permaculture set up, so that you can prevent problems from showing up and maximize yield.

2. Remember that everything in a permaculture garden should be placed in a way that speeds up workflow. Keep ease of access in mind when you're designing the layout and don't hesitate to move certain components of your design around to find the best fit.

3. Maximize crop yield by following the tips outlined in Chapter 5. Growing perennials, building raised beds and growing companion plants are some surefire ways to keep your kitchen full throughout the year.

4. Think of creative ways to utilize space. Raised beds and growing vegetable vines on trellises are some good ideas to maximize space. They are also excellent structures for patios or terraces.

5. Focus on generating profits and use them to benefit your community by investing in local small businesses.

6. Setting up a successful permaculture garden ultimately comes down to having fun. So enjoy working on your little garden patch or piece of land. Learn from your mistakes and have fun growing your favorite plants.

"I grow plants for many reasons: to please my eye or to please my soul, to challenge the elements or to challenge my patience, for novelty or for nostalgia, but mostly for the joy in seeing them grow."

– David Hobson (Author of A Diary of A Mad Gardener)

CONCLUSION:

Permaculture and Economic Livelihoods

Permaculture offers a unique opportunity for people from all different walks of life to observe the wisdom of the natural world and to design landscapes and lifestyles that are healthy, regenerative, and abundant. Producing your own food is often the first step towards reclaiming your autonomy, improving your health, creating a deeper sense of community, and living a fuller life. While all of these are certainly important goals and outcomes, permaculture can also play an important role in helping people to escape the "rat race" and live more economically independent lives. Unfortunately, too many people are stuck in situations where they live "paycheck to paycheck" with little time, energy, and resources to dedicate to making their permaculture dream design come to life.

In purely practical terms, a quality permaculture design can help you achieve a healthier economic livelihood in the following ways:

- **Avoid a Mortgage**
  Though we didn't talk in this book about how permaculture and natural building techniques are related, your home is "zone 0." Permaculture offers an abundance of ideas for how to use earthen building techniques to build a healthy, sustainable home for a minimum budget. Building a home from the mud beneath our feet or from timber might allow some people to avoid the long-term debt that comes with mortgages.

- **Reduce Your Bills**
  Even if you don't build your own cob or adobe home, permaculture design principles can also help you to radically reduce those dreaded monthly bills. A quality zone and sector analysis can help you determine different landscaping strategies to reduce your home's heating and cooling bills. For example, you can make use of photovoltaic cells to meet your energy requirements. By recycling your gray water into a backyard wetland or mini food forest, you may also be able to cut back on your water bills. Another tip is to plant a deciduous tree to the south of your house to provide shade in the summer while still allowing the sun to warm your house in the winter. If you need a fast-growing option you could consider the nitrogen-fixing "black locust" which also provides excellent rott-resistant wood for fences, trellises, and construction.

- **Grow Your Own Food**
  The average person in the United States spends almost $8,000 each year on food expenses. Growing a portion of your own food, then, is also a simple way to quickly save money.

- **Sell Your Surplus**
  Lastly, and perhaps most importantly, a quality permaculture design will quickly begin to yield benefits in

the form of an amazing production of healthy, organic food products. The bumper crop of tomatoes and zucchinis from your backyard hügelkultur bed will most likely be much more than you could ever eat, and selling your excess produce is a great way to add a bit of income. More and more consumers are ready to pay premium prices for organic food products. Once you begin to experience the abundance that permaculture design begins to offer, you might find that permaculture can offer a sustainable source of income as well.

In many ways, permaculture is the future. Sooner or later, all of us have to find more sustainable ways of living as the Earth's resources dwindle. Permaculture is all about returning to our roots and living in ways that are similar to our ancestors' way of life. It involves honoring nature and working together with different elements to create a sustainable agricultural system. With climate change posing a serious threat to our existence on this planet, I believe that permaculture will soon turn into a necessity rather than an option.

My aim is to help you achieve the freedom you've always desired. I want you to feel empowered knowing that you are in control of your food supply. I want nothing more than to hear you say that you feel confident in your ability to feed your family regardless of the circumstances.

While the ultimate goal may be to be food-sufficient and independent, try to enjoy the process. Observe the changes in seasons, the flowers blossoming, the ripening leaves falling off trees and moving to your compost pile, your cucumbers turning into pickles and your apples into jams. Watch the birds enjoying the fruits of your labor and bees helping you with your work.

I believe permaculture offers so much more than healthy food and self-reliance. It offers a closer relationship with nature and the awareness of our place in the natural order of things. We are a part of nature and it is time that we remember that.

...something important...

Free Goodwill – The Power of Giving Back

"Though the problems of the world are increasingly complex, the solution remains embarrassingly simple."
– Bill Mollison

People who help others with zero expectations experience higher levels of happiness, live longer and feel their life to be meaningful. Permaculture aims to make sure that everyone has access to the resources that are necessary for creating a better life. I believe in the power of goodwill and giving back, and I love to see as it builds trust and cooperation between people.

I'd like to create the opportunity to deliver this value to you while you are reading or listening to this book. To do so, I have a simple question for you. Would you help someone you've never met if it wouldn't cost you any money, but you'd never get credit for your kindness?

If so, I'd have an ask to make on behalf of someone you do not know and likely never will. They are just like you, or you were a few years ago: less experienced, full of desires to help the world, seeking information but not sure where to look.

That's the point where you can add your part. The only way for me to accomplish my mission of spreading information about permaculture and self-sustainability for these searching people is first by reaching them. And most people do, in fact, just judge a book by its cover and reviews.

If you have found this book valuable, please take a brief moment right now and leave an honest review of the book and its content. It will cost you zero dollars and takes less than sixty seconds.

I have committed myself to plant a tree with a Forest Garden Program in Senegal/Africa after every single review that pops up for the book. With our trees, new forest gardens will rejuvenate the region, as well as create food security and revenue for the local farmers. So you and I can make a real difference:

- Your review will help one more person to put healthy food on their family's table.

- Your review will help one more family who are doing work they find meaningful.

- Your review will help one more fellow gardener experience a transformation that other farmers have never encountered.

- Your review will help one more life change for the better.

- Your review can help change the world.

To make this happen, all you have to do is leave a review.

Just scan this QR code with your phone, or visit https://review.sophiemckay.com to do it.

You can follow the "Plant a Tree Project" on my homepage, at www.sophiemckay.com.

Thank you so much. Your support means the world to me.

Your biggest fan, *Sophie*

What to Read Next?

If You Liked This Book, Try This One Too!

Sophie's fantastic new book, **The Beginner's Guide to Successful Container Gardening**, is now published!

Inside, **you will learn about the basics of container gardening**, including **selecting the right container, soil, and plants** for all your needs. You will also learn about the specific requirements of different types of plants, and how to care for them throughout the growing season. **Whether you're a seasoned gardener or just getting started, this book has something for everyone.**

So if you're ready for some more inspiration, check out this book now to keep your garden thriving all year round with **25+ proven DIY methods for composting, companion planting, seed saving, water management and pest control!**

So what are you waiting for? Grab it for yourself!

Just **scan this QR code** with your phone, or visit the

https://Container.SophieMckay.com link to land directly on the book's Amazon page.

BIBLIOGRAPHY

Bailey, P. (n.d.). *10 benefits of urban permaculture*. Agritecture. Retrieved October 31, 2021, from https://www.agritecture.com/blog/2019/5/28/10-benefits-of-urban-permaculture

Berry, W. (1969). *The Long-Legged House*.

Berry, W. (1977). *The Unsettling of America: Culture and Agriculture*. Sierra Club Book.

Brown, C. W. (n.d.). *Raised beds*. Permaculture Association. https://www.permaculture.org.uk/practical-solutions/raised-beds#:~:text=Raised%20beds%20have%20numerous%20benefits,soil%20and%20prevent%20soil%20compaction.

Constantini, N. W., Arieli, R., Chodick, G., & Dubnov-Raz, G. (2010, September). High prevalence of vitamin D insufficiency in athletes and dancers. *Clinical Journal of Sports Medicine, 20*(5), 368 - 371. 10.1097/JSM.0b013e3181f207f2

Davis, D. R., Epp, M. D., & Riordan, H. D. (2005, December). Changes in USDA food composition data for 43 garden crops, 1950 to 1999. *Journal of the American College of Nutrition, 23*(6), 669 - 682. 10.1080/07315724.2004.10719409

Dowding, C. (2019, September 26). *No-dig Gardening*. Joe Gardener. Retrieved February 6, 2022, from https://joegardener.com/podcast/no-dig-gardening-charles-dowding/

Duvauchelle, J. (n.d.). *Advantages & Disadvantages of Raised Beds*. Home Guides. Retrieved December 27, 2021, from

https://homeguides.sfgate.com/advantages-disadvantages-raised-beds-99753.html

Eng, M. (2013, July 10). *Most produce loses 30 percent of nutrients three days after harvest*. Chicago Tribune. Retrieved October 31, 2021, from https://www.chicagotribune.com/dining/ct-xpm-2013-07-10-chi-most-produce-loses-30-percent-of-nutrients-three-days-after-harvest-20130710-story.html

Engels, J. (2017, September 22). *The Basics of Growing Food in the Winter - The Permaculture Research Institute*. Permaculture Research Institute. Retrieved November 22, 2021, from

https://www.permaculturenews.org/2017/09/22/basics-growing-food-winter/

Environmental Protection Agency. (n.d.). *Climate Impacts on Agriculture and Food Supply*. Environmental Protection Agency. Retrieved November 7, 2021, from https://19january2017snapshot.epa.gov/climate-impacts/climate-impacts-agriculture-and-food-supply_.html

Fairfield, K. M., & Fletcher, R. H. (2002, June 19). Vitamins for Chronic Disease Prevention in Adults: Scientific Review. *Journal of American Medical Association, 287*(23), 3116 - 3126. 10.1001/jama.287.23.3116

Fukuoka, M. (1978). *The One-straw Revolution: An Introduction to Natural Farming*. Rodale Press.

Gasnier, C., Dumont, C., Benachour, N., Clair, E., Chagnon, M.-C., & Séralini, G.-E. (2009, August 21). Glyphosate-based herbicides are toxic and endocrine disruptors in human cell lines. *Toxicology, 262*(3), 184 - 191. 10.1016/j.tox.2009.06.006

Indoor Plants. (n.d.). Deep Green Permaculture. Retrieved January 2, 2022, from https://deepgreenpermaculture.com/indoor-plants/

Jackson, W. (2011). *Nature as measure: the selected essays of Wes Jackson*. Counterpoint Press.

Jacques, K. (n.d.). *How to Make Compost Tea | Almanac.com*. The Old Farmer's Almanac. Retrieved December 12, 2021, from https://www.almanac.com/content/how-make-compost-tea#

Jenkins, E. (2018, September 24). *How to Make Your Permaculture Garden Work in Off-Seasons • New Life On A Homestead*. New Life On A Homestead. Retrieved November 22, 2021, from

https://www.newlifeonahomestead.com/make-permaculture-garden-work-in-off-seasons/

Kaidar-Person, O., Person, B., Szomstein, S., & Rosenthal, R. J. (2008, July). Nutritional deficiencies in morbidly obese patients: a new form of malnutrition? Part A: vitamins. *Journal of Obesity Surgery, 18*(7), 870-876. 10.1007/s11695-007-9349-y

King, F. H. (1911). *Farmers of Forty Centuries; Or, Permanent Agriculture in China, Korea and Japan*. Dover Publications.

Mollison, B. (1988). *Permaculture: A Designer's Manual* (7th ed.). Tagari Publications.

Morrow, R. (2006). *Earth User's Guide to Permaculture* (2nd ed.). Permanent Publications.

National Center for Home Food Preservation (2017). *How Do I? Can*. Retrieved February 6, 2022, from

https://nchfp.uga.edu/how/general/ensuring_safe_canned_foods.html

Peixoto, F. (2005, December). Comparative effects of the Roundup and glyphosate on mitochondrial oxidative phosphorylation. *Chemosphere, 61*(8), 1115 - 1122. 10.1016/j.chemosphere.2005.03.044

Post, S. G. (2005). Altruism, happiness, and health: it's good to be good. International Journal of Behavioral Medicine, 12(2). 10.1207/s15327558ijbm1202_4.

Quinn, D. (1999). *Beyond Civilization: Humanity's Next Great Adventure*.

Roberts, T. (2017, September 21). *The Benefits of Creating Wetlands on Your Farm - The Permaculture Research Institute*. Permaculture Research Institute. Retrieved December 12, 2021, from https://www.permaculturenews.org/2017/09/21/benefits-creating-wetlands-farm/

Roberts, T. (2017, October 13). *A Primer on Creating Soil - The Permaculture Research Institute*. Permaculture Research Institute. Retrieved December 12, 2021, from https://www.permaculturenews.org/2017/10/13/primer-creating-soil/

Roberts, T. (2017, October 22). *The Importance of Guilds and Nitrogen Fixers - The Permaculture Research Institute*. Permaculture Research

Institute. Retrieved December 27, 2021, from https://www.permaculturenews.org/2017/10/22/importance-guilds-nitrogen-fixers/

Roberts, T. (2017, November 29). *Water Saving Irrigation Practices - The Permaculture Research Institute*. Permaculture Research Institute. Retrieved December 13, 2021, from https://www.permaculturenews.org/2017/11/29/water-saving-irrigation-practices/

Rollins, C. A., & Ingham, E. R. (2008). *Adding Biology - For Soil and Hydroponic Systems*. Nature Technologies International & Sustainable Studies.

Sepp Holzer's Permaculture: A Practical Guide to Small-Scale, Integrative Farming and Gardening. (2011). Chelsea Green Publishing.

Roundup Revealed: Glyphosate in Our Food System. (2017, June 6). As You Sow. Retrieved February 5, 2022, from

https://www.asyousow.org/reports/roundup-revealed-glyphosate-in-our-food-system

Shehata, A. A., Schrödl, W., Aldin, A. A., Hafez, H. M., & Krüger, M. (2013, April). The effect of glyphosate on potential pathogens and beneficial members of poultry microbiota in vitro. *Current Microbiology, 66*(4), 350 - 358. 10.1007/s00284-012-0277-2

Stout, R. (n.d.). *Ruth Stout's System*. Mother Earth News. Retrieved November 28, 2021, from https://www.motherearthnews.com/organic-gardening/ruth-stouts-system-zmaz04fmzsel

Thompson, R. (2018). Gardening for health: a regular dose of gardening. *Clinical Medicine, 18*(3). 10.7861/clinmedicine.18-3-201

Toensmeier, E. (2013, January 24). *Integrating Livestock in the Food Forest - The Permaculture Research Institute*. Permaculture Research Institute. Retrieved December 13, 2021, from

https://www.permaculturenews.org/2013/01/24/integrating-livestock-in-the-food-forest/

Toensmeier, E., Ferguson, R., & Mehra, M. (2020, July 10). Perennial vegetables: A neglected resource for biodiversity, carbon sequestration, and nutrition. *PLOS ONE, 15* (7), https://doi.org/10.1371/journal.pone.0234611

Printed in Great Britain
by Amazon

19806124R00092